Praise for *Finding the Space to Lead*

"At the World Economic Forum, I saw in person how Janice Marturano's mindful leadership training could make a real difference in the lives of corporate leaders from around the globe. Her powerful new book, *Finding the Space to Lead*, makes the principles of this training accessible to readers everywhere. Whether you're the leader of a corporation or a PTA or you just find yourself overwhelmed by the pace of modern life, you will find both invaluable wisdom and practical advice in these pages."

—**Arianna Huffington, president and editor-in-chief, Huffington Post Media Group**

"Mindful Leadership has transformed my life. As a corporate change agent my ability to understand myself and others better is crucial to bring about skillful and sustainable improvements. In *Finding the Space to Lead*, Janice—the pioneer of mindful leadership—offers us the practices that have enriched my own leadership competencies and opened the most meaningful workplace and life dimensions."

—**Andreas Metzen, senior vice president, DVB Bank SE**

"I describe my first mindfulness retreat as life-changing and once again Janice has wowed me. Her clarity, encouragement, and reminders to be gentle on ourselves as we learn to be mindful leaders are simply amazing. *Finding the Space to Lead* will benefit all who read and practice it."

—**Gale S. Pollock, major general (ret.), CRNA, FACHE, FAAN**

"Janice Marturano knows what leadership excellence is, and shows us how it can be cultivated. Much more than just a simple application of some mindfulness techniques, *Finding the Space to*

Lead joins mind training exercises and sound business disciplines into practical, transformative leadership practices."

—**James Gimian, publisher,**
***Mindful* magazine and Mindful.org**

"Janice Marturano has been an inspiration to many of her friends at General Mills. Her new book, which explores the framework of mindful leadership, is an excellent read for anyone balancing the complexities of modern life and leadership."

—**Michael L. Davis, executive vice president,**
human resources, General Mills

"This is a book filled with practical steps that can help businesses to succeed by cultivating the strengths of their most important resource—their employees. This book is a must read for business leaders who want to create a sustainable corporate environment grounded in shared communication and trust."

—**Matt Mumber, M.D., author of *Sustainable Wellness: An***
Integrative Approach to Transform Your Mind, Body, and Spirit

"With leaders everywhere searching for ways to be mindful, Janice Marturano's timely new book, *Finding the Space to Lead*, is the definitive guide to becoming a mindful leader. If you follow her practical advice and easy-to-adopt exercises, this book will change your life. You will not only become a better leader, you will have a more fulfilling life."

—**Bill George, professor, Harvard Business School,**
and former chair and CEO, Medtronic

"A must read for anyone in a leadership position. This is a riveting account of how mindfulness can transform leadership in organizations and improve individual well-being and organizational success. Sprinkled with compelling real-world examples, this book should be required reading for leaders of any organization."

—Richard J. Davidson, founder and chair, Center for Investigating Healthy Minds, University of Wisconsin-Madison

"We live in a world where every single person is a leader in some capacity and everyone is trying to figure out how to deal with the increasing demands and complexities of life. *Finding the Space to Lead* gives us concrete strategies, from a high powered executive of a major American corporation, to increase our focus and creativity, as well as how to lead with compassion. In this practical and straightforward book, Janice Marturano shares her down to earth and common sense approach that can help moms and moguls alike. I highly recommend it."

—Congressman Tim Ryan, Ohio, author of *A Mindful Nation*

"Janice Marturano is a widely-admired executive and a leader in a movement that is changing the shape of our world through mindfulness and emotional intelligence. With this insightful book, leaders of all shapes and sizes will not only become much more effective in every way, they will also become happier."

—Chade-Meng Tan, Google's Jolly Good Fellow and international bestselling author of *Search Inside Yourself*

"Janice's personal story about discovering mindfulness, and ultimately defining how it applies to enhanced leadership, is inspiring. This is not some 'new age mindset' rhetoric . . . As someone who had no idea what mindfulness was, this has made me a better leader, father, and husband by building the muscle of staying focused 'on demand.'"

—Joe Ens, vice president, General Mills

"This book is both deeply moving and utterly inspiring. Whether you are already a leader, or are preparing to lead, or perhaps you have had leadership 'thrust upon you,' reading this book and following its practices will become a lifeline, allowing you to discover a way to cultivate your deepest potential to lead with excellence and wisdom."

—Mark Williams, professor of
clinical psychology, University of Oxford

"Janice Marturano has walked the path of leadership and knows its challenges firsthand. In Finding the Space to Lead, she outlines a focused approach to those challenges using the skills of moment-to-moment awareness. The practices contained here will do more than change you as a leader; they will reacquaint you with yourself."

—Pat Barrick, vice president, City Harvest

Finding the Space to Lead

A Practical Guide to Mindful Leadership

by Janice Marturano

BLOOMSBURY PRESS
NEW YORK · LONDON · OXFORD · NEW DELHI · SYDNEY

This book is dedicated to those who aspire to lead
with courage, integrity, and compassion.

Bloomsbury Press
An imprint of Bloomsbury Publishing Plc

1385 Broadway	50 Bedford Square
New York	London
NY 10018	WC1B 3DP
USA	UK

www.bloomsbury.com

BLOOMSBURY and the Diana logo are trademarks of Bloomsbury Publishing Plc

First published 2014

ISBN: HB: 978-1-62040-247-4
         ePub: 978-1-62040-248-1

Library of Congress Cataloging-in-Publication Data

Marturano, Janice.
Finding the space to lead : a practical guide to leadership excellence through
mindfulness / by Janice Marturano.—First Edition.
pages cm
Includes bibliographical references and index.
ISBN 978-1-62040-247-4 (alk. Paper hardcover)
1. Leadership—Psychological aspects. 2. Meditation. I. Title.
BF637.L4M287 2014
658.4'092—dc23
2013031415

4 6 8 10 9 7 5

Typeset by Westchester Book Group
Printed and bound in the U.S.A. by Berryville Graphics, Berryville, Virginia

To find out more about our authors and books visit www.bloomsbury.com.
Here you will find extracts, author interviews, details of forthcoming
events, and the option to sign up for our newsletters.

Bloomsbury books may be purchased for business or promotional use.
For information on bulk purchases please contact Macmillan Corporate and
Premium Sales Department at specialmarkets@macmillan.com.

Contents

Introduction: Training the Mind to Cultivate Leadership Excellence

LEADING PEOPLE IS ONE OF THE most challenging roles we can take on in life. It requires a dizzying array of skills, a strong education, and passion. Most often, when we take on a leadership role, we do so because we want to make a difference. As leaders, we take for granted that we will work long hours, make great sacrifices, and ride the roller coaster of success and failure. However, the busy-ness that accompanies being a leader in today's 24/7/365 interconnected world often distracts us from what's important and limits our ability to lead with excellence. When we are really honest with ourselves, we may have to admit that there are far too many times when we feel as though we're spending the day putting out fires and wasting time rather than doing our best work.

Does it need to be this way? Happily, the answer is no.

You can learn to lead with excellence by cultivating your innate capabilities to focus on what is important, to see more clearly what is presenting itself, to foster greater creativity, and to embody compassion. When you are able to do so, you are much more likely to make the conscious choices we need our leaders to make. These choices often lead to a *win-win-win* scenario: good for the organization, good for the employees, and good for the community.

HOW I CAME TO MINDFUL LEADERSHIP

I came to mindful leadership somewhat unexpectedly while I was vice president, public responsibility and deputy general counsel at General Mills, one of the world's largest corporations. (I talk more about the circumstances that led me to mindfulness training and its transformative effect on me personally in Chapter 2.) I was leading the high-intensity life that most corporate officers—and other busy people, from ministers to moms—know well, dealing with nonstop demands in the workplace and outside it. It took a personal crisis, but I discovered that mindfulness training would teach me to find more of the very thing we need most in our lives: space.

By "space," I don't mean literally more square feet in our offices (though that might help). I mean mental and emotional space—"bandwidth," to use the Internet metaphor: the capacity to see, feel, hear, and reflect on what is in front of us and what is inside of us. When we have that space, we can deal with even an urgent problem in a calm, creative, and humane way, rather than have an expedient reaction to the pressure.

I helped train first a core group of officer and director colleagues at General Mills, and later hundreds of employees throughout the organization. The leaders at General Mills, a company consistently recognized for its leadership education and corporate social responsibility, embraced the training for themselves and for their teams. Ultimately, a global demand for this training began to develop outside of General Mills, and this led me to found, in 2010, the Institute for Mindful Leadership (Institute). To date, business leaders and organizational employees from more than sixty different organizations from around the world—Fortune 500 companies, entrepreneurs, non-profit directors, military officers, academic administrators, lawyers, teachers, and healthcare professionals—have been trained using mindful leadership curricula. And in 2013, the Institute was invited to bring a mindful leadership workshop to perhaps the most prominent gathering of leaders from diverse organizations: the World Economic Forum in Davos, Switzerland.

HOW YOU CAN BENEFIT FROM TRAINING IN MINDFUL LEADERSHIP

Mindfulness is not about stress reduction or taking deep breaths. It is not a religion. It's a methodology that trains a capacity of your mind that generally receives little or no training. Just as we know that your body has innate capabilities that can be strengthened through physical training, we now know from more than three decades of research that you can also train your mind to strengthen its capabilities. *Finding the Space to Lead* will show you a way to begin this training so you can learn to lead and live with excellence.

Part 1 describes what mindful leadership is, why I started training in it and then training others, and why it is so effective in developing leadership excellence.

In Part 2, you will learn a wide variety of simple methods to cultivate your capacity to lead with excellence, including meditations, reflections, and purposeful pauses (a method to train your mind by bringing attention to routine or especially chaotic moments in the day). All of these have been tried, tested, and refined in mindful leadership workshops and retreats over the past several years. Many of the meditations and reflections are also available in audio and can be accessed by going to the *Finding the Space to Lead* website (www.FindingtheSpacetoLead.com).

In Part 3, you will be invited to take the training into applications and questions for contemplation that will help you evolve from a manager who is good at execution to a leader who consistently makes a difference.

Appendix 1 contains an index of all of the meditations, purposeful pauses, and reflections used in *Finding the Space to Lead*, so you can quickly refer to any one that you would like to practice at any given time. In Appendix 2, you will find an easy-to-follow sample approach for developing a personalized program using the elements described in this book. And throughout the book, there are stories from leaders whose lives have been touched by mindful leadership training. All of the stories are authentic although the names of people and organizations have been changed to preserve privacy and business confidentiality.

We all have the potential to lead with excellence, and we simply can no longer afford to make decisions and choices without bringing all of our capabilities to the people, issues, or opportunities at hand. Of course, it takes more than good intentions to be able to change the overconnected, distracted way we go through much of our lives.

We need to train the mind's innate capabilities to notice when we are on autopilot or becoming distracted by thoughts of the past or the future, and then to redirect our full attention to whom and what we are encountering in this moment. When the mind is trained to be fully attentive, even in the midst of chaos, we have the space to make more wise and conscious choices. Whether you are leading a global organization, a small partnership, a team of colleagues, a hospital, a community group, or a family, *Finding the Space to Lead* will help you do just that.

What Is Mindful Leadership?

CHAPTER 1

Leading in the Midst of Chaos

Opportunities for leadership are all around us. The capacity for leadership is deep within us.

SECRETARY OF STATE MADELEINE ALBRIGHT

IT'S BEEN A LONG DAY, BUT YOU are finally in your car driving home. You flip on the radio to listen to the news, and amid the usual stories about the economy and the most recent skirmishes around the world, you hear the announcer mention that a national food brand is being recalled because it may contain bacteria that can cause serious gastrointestinal illness. And it involves your favorite brand of chocolate chip cookies! Now you're only partially listening to the rest of the news as your mind begins to wonder: Do I have any of those cookies in my pantry right now? Did I eat some last night? Did my son take some to school in his lunch? I was feeling a little queasy last Sunday; did I have any cookies that day?

Ever wonder how national recalls are decided? They can be some of the most challenging decisions an organization encounters. At stake are the safety of consumers, the company's hard-won reputation for quality, millions of dollars, and perhaps even some people's jobs. A decision needs to be made in a very short time, a day or so at most. When a company has clear evidence of a quality issue, the decision is simple. However, there are times when data are inconclusive and the leaders are not aligned on the decision. What then?

A couple of years ago, Jim, a veteran executive of a Fortune 500 company, told me about just such a recall. He also told me how the work that he and his team had been doing with mindful leadership played a major role in a very challenging decision-making process.

My day began like most days. Too many meetings, too many priorities, and too many potential opportunities. Then a call came in. It wasn't just any call, it was the kind of call that had the power to turn the day on its head. It erased every meeting from my calendar and demanded that I drop every other priority. A potential serious contamination issue had arisen with an important product line. When a concern about the safety of a food product emerges, I am one of three leaders of a team responsible for recommending to the CEO whether or not to recall the product. Sue, Mark, and I were seasoned executives, and we had led the team through potential recall situations before. Fortunately, these instances were rare in my company, and the team in place to handle them had been together for many years. We knew each other well, and we had great respect for each other's expertise and experience.

Within an hour of the call coming in, our recall team was equipped with data, research, and informed opinions and questions. The first step was to understand the magnitude of the problem. Unfortunately, in this case, I soon learned that an internationally distributed chocolate candy product might contain bacteria that could cause serious illness, especially for the elderly and young children.

In these situations, there is a huge amount of pressure. We were very concerned about any potential threat to the consumer's health, and we were also concerned about the potential public relations issues and the fact that a recall can cost millions of dollars and significantly damage the product's brand. The recall team began to work through what we knew, and what additional information we could obtain through testing. We notified the appropriate government agencies and advised them of the status of the investigation into the potential problem, and we gathered outside experts, microbiologists and food scientists, to help with technical questions. I knew it all had to be done in the next twenty-four to forty-eight hours. If there was a problem with our product, we would need to bring our recommendation to the CEO quickly to protect our consumers.

Generally the test results and consumer complaint information enable us to reach a consensus fairly quickly. We confirm a quality issue, or we disprove the allegation, and the decision becomes clear. It is based on analysis and facts. But it wouldn't be so simple this time. This time, despite working around the clock with the team, in hours and hours of meetings examining reams of scientific analyses and test results, we were left with only an unsubstantiated finding that the product *might be the cause of an outbreak of illness in an area of the country where food-borne illness had seen a spike and one of the possible products involved was our candy.* No conclusive data. No smoking gun. No incontrovertible evidence. This time we knew that our decision would have to be based on something more than the data and expert advice we had heard. This time Sue, Mark, and I knew that we would need to rely on our experience and intuition to reach that final decision.

In the early evening of the second day, time was running out. Sue, Mark, and I left our recall team and gathered in an empty conference room to deliberate. As we settled into our chairs, Mark suggested that we each begin with a brief monologue to share our overall analysis of the situation and our opinion on the recall. I remember feeling a sense of relief that we each had been trained in mindful communication so we were comfortable with using monologues and deep listening. And, as we began the process, I privately hoped that there would be a consensus among us. There wasn't. Now what?

One option would have been to begin a discussion about our points. You know, the kind of typical debating that can absorb enormous amounts of time and rarely results in a great choice. More often it is a compromise, or a choice that is only supported by a few of those in attendance. Too much was at stake here for that to be our next step.

So, rather than continue with a discussion, Sue suggested that we let what we had heard sink in and take some time for reflection. We agreed to reconvene in an hour. Mark left the room and took a walk around the building. Sue found a quiet, empty room in which to sit. I found a cup of coffee and returned to my office, closed the door, and allowed myself the quiet I needed to take in all that I had heard and felt during the course of the day—the quiet that would allow me to listen carefully to my intuition.

An hour later, we returned to the conference room and shared our opinions once more. This time we had reached a clear and strong consensus. It would not be a welcome decision to many in the organization, but it was now clear to the three of us that we would need to recommend a recall.

As with most difficult decisions, arriving at a clear choice was critical in Jim's story. Jim, Mark, and Sue felt more confident being able to speak with the CEO (and others) from the strong foundation and mutual support of a unanimous decision. This was a decision born not from the data, which remained inconclusive, but from their collective experience and intuition. When they took their unanimous recommendation to the CEO, he asked only one question, "Did anyone have a different point of view?" When the response was no, he quickly agreed with the recommendation. Their clarity helped the CEO as well: he could feel confident in the choice to authorize an expensive recall because all of his advisers had arrived at the same conclusion. It was the right thing to do.

Now everyone's energies could turn to the most effective and efficient ways to carry out the recall. It wasn't what anyone wanted to happen, but the decision was easier to implement and live with over the long run because they had taken the time necessary to be clear about the best choice. This was not a quick, reactive decision in the swirl of uncertainty. It was not a decision that arose from the exhaustion of a long debate. This was a choice the team leaders made using their ability to know when it was important to allow the mind to settle so that they had a better chance to discern the best choice.

As managers trained in mindful leadership, Jim, Sue, and Mark knew how to combine their traditional business and leadership skills and hard-won experience with their training of the mind. Mindful leadership practices and exercises had taught them to notice the strong pull to react, the mind's propensity to narrow the focus when under stress, the dynamics of difficult conversations that can sometimes be resolved by reaching the lowest common denominator to gain agreement rather than the most skillful choice, and the negative effects of information overload. The training also helped them choose to hold the ambiguity of "not knowing the answer" for a while, providing the quiet and spaciousness needed to see clearly and to respond. Neither their traditional business training nor mind training alone would have sufficed to help them reach an optimal decision. It's the combination of the two that proved to be so powerful.

Jim, Sue, and Mark had the courage to stop for a while, to allow the dust to settle, and to use all of their capabilities to help guide the decision. In the midst of the chaos, these leaders exhibited *leadership excellence*. All too often we are unaware of the effect that being in a pressure-filled situation has on our ability to lead with excellence. We have the innate ability to be fully present for those tough decisions—for all of our decisions—but we need to notice when we are moving into a reactive mode and learn practices that will help us make conscious choices.

Everyone has the capacity to lead with excellence. You may be in a position right now that requires you to make decisions affecting those around you and wider circles beyond—and so you consider yourself a leader and you are seen as a leader by others. Or you may not hold a leadership role per se and yet touch the lives of others every day in ways that clearly have the potential to have a leadership impact. Whatever the case, we all experience the *opportunity for leadership* referred to by Secretary Albright in the epigraph at the head of this chapter. When Secretary Albright referred to the capacity for leadership that is "deep within us," she was talking about the kind of leadership that is a potential outgrowth of mindful leadership training.

WHY DO WE NEED MINDFUL LEADERSHIP?

To answer that question, let's begin with a look at what it means to be mindful.

When you are mindful of this moment, you are present for your life and your experience just as it is . . .

> not as you hoped it would be,
> not as you expected it to be,
> not seeing more or less than what is here,
> not with judgments that can lead you to a conditioned
>   reaction
> . . . but for exactly what is here, as it unfolds, meeting each
>   moment with equanimity.

As we consider the challenges leaders face today, it's relatively easy to see how much we need to cultivate mindful leadership. The environment we live and work in is constantly evolving. Time is now often measured in Internet microseconds. There are new and complex economic and resource constraints on our organizations. We are attached 24/7 to an array of technological devices that regularly generate anxiety-producing information overload and a sense of disconnection that can overwhelm and isolate us. The world is changing so rapidly that people training for a career today may find the career path radically altered by the time they are ready to enter it. One paradigm after another is shifting. The volume of information at our disposal is, in fact, leading to less rather than more certainty. The number of voices and opinions we can hear on any given issue is so dauntingly large that we often don't know who or what to believe or follow.

It is also true, though, that these tumultuous times can offer great opportunity and ample possibilities for innovation, as the world becomes smaller and we begin to see the potential to meet the complexities of the day in ways that are truly creative, productive, and compassionate. It's a time to take leadership, and to redefine what it means to lead with excellence.

In my own experiences, first as a Wall Street associate, a community volunteer, an employee in three large organizations, and an officer of a Fortune 200 company for fifteen years, and then in the work I have done in offering mindful leadership training to leaders from around the world, I've consistently found that the best leaders' qualities go far beyond "getting the job done." The best leaders are women and men who have first-class training, bright minds, warm hearts, a passionate embrace of their mission, a strong connection to their colleagues and communities, and the courage to be open to what is here. They're driven to excellence, innovation, and making a difference.

Yet time and again, they feel as though their capabilities and their leadership training are inadequate. They tell me that even as they execute well and meet the quarterly goals, they simply do not feel they are living their best lives—at work or at home. They feel something is missing. But what?

The most frequent answer is:

Space.

We often simply do not have the space, the breathing room, necessary to be clear and focused, and to listen deeply to ourselves and to others. As we saw in Jim's story, it requires training and courage to intentionally create such space.

One of the ways people put space into their lives is by attending a mindful leadership retreat. On a recent retreat that I led, Sarah, a midcareer marketing director, described her day as "running a gauntlet." She, like many others, juggles a young family and a successful career. After one of the retreat's early-morning meditation practice sessions, she shared with the other participants that her life was filled to the brim: "I get halfway through the day and feel successful, because I think I must be accomplishing a great deal. After all, I've been running from meeting to meeting. Something useful must be happening! On top of that, I'm getting good reviews from my manager."

Later that day, as Sarah began to use the unscheduled time at the retreat to stop and take a closer look at what was happening in her day, she began to realize that there can be a big difference between a filled schedule and a full life. "I'm simply checking the boxes on the to-do list," she said, "but I'm not really there. I never have enough time to be as creative or innovative as I know I could be. And often I feel so rushed in the day that I just give a quick approval to get a project off my desk even though a part of me knows I might have contributed more to it if I had some more time."

Sarah recognized the toll that living on a nonstop treadmill can take on us. For one thing, creativity and the innovation that results from healthy collaboration often suffer: how can we expect to generate the connections with our colleagues and communities that we need when we are so busy that all we can really do is check off boxes, squeeze in a perfunctory hello to our co-workers, and get through the day's meetings and calls? Can we realistically expect leadership excellence when we spend whole days on autopilot—

looking at our watches and wondering where the day went, looking at the calendar and wondering how it could be spring when just yesterday it was Thanksgiving?

Whether our leadership affects millions, hundreds, or a handful, we can no longer afford to be on autopilot in our lives, with our families, or in our organizations. We can no longer afford to miss the connections with those we work with, those we love, and those we serve. We can no longer make decisions with distracted minds, reacting instead of responding or initiating. We can no longer lose touch with what motivated us to lead in the first place. We need mindful leadership to lead with excellence.

So far we have been exploring the need to be present for leadership roles in the workplace. There is an equally, or perhaps more, important need to be present for your leadership roles in your personal life. Excellence involves making conscious choices about not just how you work but how you live your life and how you connect with your family, friends, and community. We need mindful leadership to live with excellence.

WHAT EXACTLY IS A MINDFUL LEADER?

A mindful leader embodies leadership presence by cultivating focus, clarity, creativity, and compassion in the service of others.

Leadership presence is a tangible quality. It requires full and complete nonjudgmental attention in the present moment. Those around a mindful leader see and feel that presence.

A friend of mine decided to attend a local rally to see if he could get an important healthcare question answered by presidential candidate Bill Clinton. Of course, when he arrived, he faced a teeming, screaming crowd, but he maneuvered his way to the police barricade and waited. Clinton soon arrived and began walking along the barricade shaking hands. As my friend stretched out his hand and Clinton took it, he yelled out his question. In that moment, the candidate stopped, faced him, and responded to the question. Later my friend told me, "In those few moments when we spoke together, it seemed as though Clinton had nothing else on his mind. It was as if there was no other person there." He felt heard and respected. That's leadership presence: you give your full attention to what you're doing, and others know it.

Leadership presence is powerful. In your own life, you can probably recall times when you experienced leadership presence, either in yourself or someone else. It might have been in a one-on-one conversation, or it might have been in an audience filled with people. Presence can be felt even from far away.

You can undoubtedly recall the much more common experiences when you feel only partially in the room, or you feel the person you're speaking with is not really there. Like all of us, even when you have every intention to be focused, your mind becomes easily distracted— thinking about the past or the future, and only partially in the present if at all. In those moments, you are not embodying the innate capacity everyone possesses to be present.

Why is that? What do we know about *being present*?

As a beginning, you might recall a moment when you experienced full awareness in a situation. When there seemed to be nothing else but whatever you were noticing. This might have been a momentous moment like the birth of your child. In that moment, time seemed to stand still, and nothing else existed but the warmth of that miraculous being softly sleeping in your arms. You were not distracted by the to-do list or the noises in the hall. Your full attention—mind, body, and heart—was completely absorbed in that moment.

Or it might have been an ordinary moment, the kind often overlooked and not particularly celebrated. You may have lingered to notice a sunset. Perhaps you recall that it stopped you dead in your tracks and held you in its beauty, all of you, for what seemed like forever but in clock time might have been just a couple of seconds. In those seconds, you became aware of the shades of pink and orange, the intricate play of light and shadow, your body's absorption of the waning energy of nature, and the feeling of belonging to something bigger than yourself.

Maybe you were at the coffee shop in the morning, your mind racing through the details of the upcoming day, and you looked up from your coffee and actually noticed a piece of art on the wall or the warm, comforting aroma of the shop. Whatever it was, it interrupted the busy mind, and you were living that moment of your life more fully.

Such moments—when we fully inhabit our bodies and our senses are at work on more than an internal storyline, checklist, or rehearsed conversation—are what give life true meaning. Beyond that, for those of us who hold positions of influence, the ability to be present, to embody leadership presence, is not only critical for us as individuals, but it also has a *ripple effect* on those around us: our families and friends, the organization we work within, the community we live in, and potentially the world at large. Just as a pebble thrown into a still pond can create ripples spreading throughout the whole of the pond, so too can the cultivation of leadership presence go far beyond the effect it has on us alone.

WHEN THE INSTITUTE works with an organization to bring mindful leadership training to its employees, we witness an example of the ripple effect. We often start with retreats or courses for the more senior leaders, and as the training begins to change how they lead, those around them notice the change and soon ask to enroll in the training as well. It's not unusual to hear people tell stories of the transformation they noticed in their manager. As one person described it, "I'm here on retreat because when I asked my manager how she seems to always make me feel as though I'm important and what I have to say is valuable, even when I know she is swamped with work, she suggested I explore mindful leadership. So, here I am." As leaders we know that we often underestimate the impact, for better or worse, that we have on those around us. When we are present and engaged, the effect is very different from when we are distracted and on autopilot. But it isn't enough to *want* to be more present, to *want* to have a positive ripple effect. We need to train the mind.

The work of developing leadership presence through mindfulness begins by recognizing how much time we spend in a mental state that has come to be called *continuous partial attention*. If you're like most of us, you probably take pride in your ability to multitask, to be incredibly efficient by simultaneously listening to a conference call, writing a few e-mails, and eating your salad at your desk.

Sound familiar to you? And yet, when you were listening in on the call, did you actually hear anything? Did you share your best thinking in the e-mails? Did you enjoy your lunch, or even notice that you ate it?

Perhaps one of my most memorable lessons about the cost of multitasking came early one morning as I sat at my desk, getting things ready for a day filled with meetings and reviewing the latest e-mails. One of the messages that morning came from my husband, who was forwarding an e-mail from my daughter's teacher. It was asking us to choose one of the available parent-teacher conference slots on her calendar, and my husband wanted to know which one I wanted before he replied. I wrote to my husband, "Thursday at 10 would be great . . . love you forever, thanks for last night." Fine. Except that in my haste and partial attention, I wrote those words to my daughter's teacher. Needless to say, when I finally realized what happened, it became a moment to remember.

No harm there, just some relatively minor embarrassment. Of course, those of us who have been in the workforce for any period of time can point to almost daily e-mails containing errors and incomplete, hastily organized thoughts of dubious merit.

A few moments of people-watching in the hallways at work or

on the sidewalk in front of your building can also give you a taste of the disconnection that results from multitasking. You'll notice people texting and checking e-mails as they walk, barely avoiding walking into walls and each other. It has even become acceptable to do this when walking—and supposedly having a conversation—with someone else. Once upon a time, this would have been considered rude. Putting manners aside, though, continuous partial attention can also be exhausting and inefficient. Neuroscience is now showing us that the mind's capacity for multitasking is extremely limited. We're really built for doing one thing at a time.

The hallways of offices used to be places for informal greetings and impromptu conversations. Valuable connections could be made in the hallways. Physiologically, a walk down the hallway used to allow a few moments of space when you could leave behind the thoughts of the last meeting and arrive at the next with a bit of openness. Today, few if any connections are made, as everyone rushes down the hall with thumbs blazing on smartphones. As a result, everyone arrives at the next meeting still attached to the last one.

We lead hurried, fractured, complex lives, and we seem to be more easily losing the richness and engagement that come from being in the present moment. With all the many ways we are enticed to get distracted, to drown out our intuition, and to fragment our attention, we can easily go through our entire lives without ever bringing all of our capabilities and attention to any given moment.

WHAT DO WE do about that? Is leadership presence a natural gift possessed by a special few, or can it be cultivated? Can we train our minds to support our intention to live life with focus, clarity, creativity, and compassion even when our lives are hurried, fractured, and complex?

Thankfully, we can.

Leading with excellence, being fully present for what we do, and connecting with others—these are innate abilities we all possess. In my experience, those who are good leaders, and those who aspire to be good leaders, are eager to cultivate these abilities. Mindful leadership training can do just that. By following simple practices that hone your attention and your ability to be aware of what's going on in your body and mind at any given moment, you can utilize all of your capabilities—clear minds and warm hearts and wise choices—and begin to see the results of leading from an authentic place.

A FIRST TASTE OF MINDFUL LEADERSHIP TRAINING

Try an experiment to begin to become familiar with the activity of your mind. Right now, sit comfortably, close your eyes, and notice that you are breathing. Simply feel the breath in your body. Just that much. That's the only task on the to-do list. There's nothing to change about the breath; just feel the sensations as it enters and leaves the body. Try this for just five minutes. Sustain attention on the sensations.

What did you notice?

If you are like most of us, what seems to be a simple task was not that simple. Did you notice your mind jumping around from thought to thought even when you wanted to sustain attention on the sensations?

With practice, noticing the sensations of the breath can be a valuable anchor to bring you back to the present, even in the midst of a chaotic meeting or a difficult conversation when the mind might otherwise be filled with distractions. The sensations of your breath are only felt in the present, not the past and not the future. So, if you can intentionally focus your attention on your breath sensations for a couple of breaths, the mind returns from its worries about the future or its memories of the past to be right here, in this moment.

What you will begin to see as you cultivate your ability to be present is that the distractions that often fill your mind can cloud out the clarity you need to help guide a situation, create space for innovation, or make the connections necessary to be open to the need for compassion.

Although the many ways we are distracted by technology and the 24/7 flow of information seem to encourage our attention to be more and more fractured, and anywhere but in the present, the mind's capacity to aim and sustain attention is always available to be cultivated. In this guide to mindful leadership, you will learn the many ways that you can train the mind and bring this training into the everyday challenges of leading and living in today's world.

A NOTE ABOUT MINDFULNESS, STRESS, AND HEALTH

While the primary aim of bringing mindfulness to our leadership practices and habits is not to improve our physical health and well-being, the personal experiences of many thousands of mindfulness practitioners—as well as the results of numerous studies—have demonstrated that our health does improve in a variety of ways. The shorthand phrase for the health benefits of mindfulness practice is "stress reduction."

What we call stress is a complex system within our body and mind, and we need stress to respond effectively to challenges, threats, and emergencies. But when our body and mind are in a constant state of high stress reactivity, it takes its toll. One of the key health benefits of mindfulness is that it helps us better regulate for ourselves our stress response. In addition, increased awareness of the condition of our body and mind can influence us to make better lifestyle choices that can improve our long-term health.

A number of researchers have also concluded that mindfulness practice makes us more resilient—better able to weather the challenges of life with increased equanimity. A study conducted by Jon Kabat-Zinn and Richard Davidson showed that workers at a Wisconsin biotech firm who took part in a mindfulness program exhibited brain activity that indicated they faced challenges with less reactivity, which naturally leads to "lower stress." If in the face of a challenge, you are able to approach it more calmly, rather than overreact, your health is bound to improve. Naturally, these positive effects on our physical health and overall well-being contribute to our ability to lead with excellence.

CHAPTER 2

Finding the Space to Lead

You must learn to be still in the midst of activity and to be vibrantly alive in repose.

INDIRA GANDHI

IT WAS THE TURN OF THE CENTURY, the new millennium was dawning, and I, like many others, was continuing to hone my craft as an expert juggler. Not the juggler from the circus but the multitasking juggler. Keeping all the balls in my life in the air was an art form that required quick movements and careful balance. These balls included various roles:

Spouse—married (and thankfully still am) to my college sweetheart

Mother—two wonderful children, then aged ten and fifteen

Executive—vice president and deputy general counsel of General Mills

Daughter—very close relationship to aging parents

Community volunteer—president of the board of a major nonprofit organization in my community

My life was very full and very, very busy, but I somehow felt it was moving along as it should. Then a new ball was added. Not just any ball but a big ball, a medicine-ball-sized ball.

General Mills had decided to acquire the Pillsbury Company, in what was essentially a merger of equal-sized companies, and I had been asked to lead the antitrust clearance efforts required by the Federal Trade Commission. Although this assignment started out as a typical deal—and I had led many acquisitions in the past—it would turn into a crazy nightmare. Instead of taking the usual four to five months, this deal was so complex it would require nearly eighteen months to complete. The saga of exactly why what should have been a relatively simple clearance process dragged on for so long is worthy of its own book. For now, it is only relevant to know that the process required twelve- or fourteen-hour days for many months and that everyone at both companies was waiting and growing more anxious by the day. I often arrived at my office in the dawning light and left long after dark.

One Monday morning, as I was walking from my car to the office, my mind already fixated on the many meetings I would have that day, I bumped into an officer from Pillsbury. He asked how things were going, and when I told him about the many challenges we had been dealing with, he said, "You know, if you can't get this deal approved, ten thousand Pillsbury workers will likely lose their jobs."

His words stayed with me throughout the deal. Those ten thousand jobs meant ten thousand families to me, and I didn't want them to feel that hardship. His words only added extra weight to the pressure I already felt from this assignment. As the months wore on, the ball became heavier and heavier. The medicine ball was now a boulder. It was too big to juggle. It dominated my life.

Then, six months into the clearance process, while I was just managing to keep things in some kind of rickety balance, my mother died. The very ground beneath my feet was shaken by this event. She had been quite ill, and I knew we would not have her with us for long, but I wasn't prepared for the actual moment of her death. I'm not sure any of us are prepared for moments like that. With no one else at the company who could step in, and as a distraction from the pain I was feeling, a day after the funeral I went right back to working at a grueling pace on the merger.

Then things took another difficult turn. Just six months after my mom's death, I found myself preparing for my father's memorial service, in a daze. His death had been sudden; he passed away on the operating table due to complications from surgery. I felt the already shaky ground shake even more: both of my parents dead within six months of each other, and no time to really grieve the loss of people who had been central to my life and the values that I lived by.

I was on edge, and truth be told, some parts of my life were definitely not getting the kind of attention they needed. Somehow, finally, the Pillsbury deal went through, the acquisition occurred, and the mass layoffs were averted. At last.

Now, I thought, *I'll be able to bounce back to my regular act. Now I'll be able to sleep through the night again, to regain some of the twenty pounds I had lost without trying. Now I'll be able to heal from the scars of losing my parents.*

But it didn't happen.

Even as I began to help the two companies merge themselves into one and started working somewhat more normal hours, I still couldn't regain the energy and strength that had been drained away during those months. With almost no rest at all and no tending to the deep emotions surrounding my parents' death, I was right back at it. I was juggling again. That's what successful, hardworking achievers do. We go right back in the game. We play hurt. We're praised for it.

Yet some part of me was missing, and I didn't know how to get it back. I would later come to understand that so much mental energy had been depleted that my resiliency level was basically at zero.

DISCOVERING MINDFULNESS

A very good physician friend of mine saw beneath my daily smile, and one day he suggested that what I really needed was to go to a spa for a week, to have someone take care of me, to eat healthy food, to get massages, and to sleep for long stretches of time. The next day, he sent me an e-mail with the latest Zagat survey of the best spas in the country. At the top of the list was Miraval, in Arizona. When I opened the link, I found a beautiful resort in the desert offering pampering and a wide array of classes and services. It looked wonderful. Of course, I couldn't even imagine going home to my family with the news that I was going on vacation without them. I'd already had to send them on vacation without me at a critical point of the deal, and I didn't want to be away again. So I couldn't go.

As I took one last look at the Miraval website, though, I noticed a special program being advertised as an intensive retreat for executives on "the power of mindfulness," taught by Jon Kabat-Zinn. I had never heard of Jon, but the idea of training the mind was intriguing, so I looked further into what this mindfulness stuff was all about.

I'm not the New Age type. Far from it. I was a corporate vice president working for General Mills. I wasn't living down by the beach in Baja. I lived in Minnesota. I did love looking at the tree outside my office, but I wasn't about to get barefoot and dance around it with flowers in my hair. If I was going to take six days of training at a spa, I wanted to be sure that it was going to be worth the time.

I found some research on the effectiveness of something called Mindfulness-Based Stress Reduction—and it was compelling. I learned further that the developer of that program was the very person who would be leading the training, and that he was a microbiologist with a doctorate from the Massachusetts Institute of Technology. With those facts, I felt pretty assured that this experience would be grounded in science and not New Age slogans and clichés. After speaking with my family about it, and getting their resounding support, I signed up for the program.

It turned out to be unlike anything I had ever experienced, and I still count it among the ten most difficult things I have ever done. It began with Jon telling the twelve of us sitting in a circle that we would be sitting and meditating for about forty-five minutes. I still remember the thoughts going through my head at that moment: *Did he just say forty-five minutes of sitting still?! Why does it need to be that long? I'm not going to train my mind this week, I'm going to go crazy!*

Interestingly, I also have a vivid memory of the last day of the program, carrying my little meditation cushion to the kiva where we would meet for an early-morning practice, and thinking, *It will only be an hour. That's not nearly long enough.*

In between those two contrasting moments—the before-and-after picture of my first foray into mindfulness—I began to learn what it is like to train the mind to be in the present moment. I learned that most of us spend our entire lives distracting ourselves and thinking so much about our past and our future that we end up missing the present moment, the only moment we have to live and the only moment we can affect.

After multitasking and trying to balance all the different demands of my life, after going at a runner's pace for so many years—and at such intensity for those eighteen months—stopping and learning to be in the present felt like hitting a brick wall. Over the days of exploring mindfulness, I slowly began discovering and rediscovering my mind's innate capacity to be present, and with that discovery I began to reconnect with who I was—mind and body and heart. Slowly some mental resiliency was developing.

When I returned home, my wonderful husband met me at the door and immediately knew something had changed. I was more open and rested and at peace than I had been for a long time. I continued my daily meditation practice and began to notice those times in my day when I was not being mindful. For example, I would catch myself thinking about tomorrow's meeting instead of listening to the meeting I was attending, or I would check e-mails over lunch at my desk and realize I had no idea what my soup tasted like. On the other hand, on occasion, I began to notice that my typical reaction to a person or situation could be stopped short by my ability to use my practice to create a little space for me to consciously make another choice. It became a fascinating exploration of my own conditioning and the potential to expand my mind's capabilities.

In those first years, I was a closet meditator. I was fairly sure that most of my colleagues would not understand why I was meditating. In fact, I was pretty sure that some would not like the idea that one of the organization's senior lawyers was becoming one of those stereotypical laid-back, always calm meditation folks. Lawyers need to be edgy and assertive. My colleagues' lack of knowledge about mindfulness training might lead them to wonder if meditating would translate into losing my drive and commitment.

As I continued to develop a daily meditation practice, I wanted to learn more. I signed up for an alumni retreat for those initially trained by Jon at his Power of Mindfulness program. It was led by Saki Santorelli, the executive director of the Center for Mindfulness in Medicine, Health Care, and Society at the University of Massachusetts Medical School.

Meeting Saki began a multiyear journey during which we developed a variety of close relationships. He shared his mindfulness wisdom and experience and helped me significantly deepen my practice, and he taught me the art of teaching mindfulness. I agreed to join the advisory board of the Center for Mindfulness, became its director of leadership education, and offered my skills as a trained strategist to support the center. We became colleagues and friends, and together we would develop the first mindful leadership curriculum and co-lead mindful leadership retreats for almost five years. It was a full and rich training ground for my practice and for what would eventually become a major change in my life.

Meanwhile, at General Mills, I was increasingly noticing that my mindfulness practice was making me a better leader. Simultaneously, I was becoming increasingly aware of the strain that was showing in my friends and colleagues, and those I worked with in other sectors of society. It was, and still is, incredibly difficult to lead with excellence. Those people were working very hard and feeling exhausted, and they were also feeling frustrated, because they didn't have the time or space needed to offer the kind of creative solutions, mentoring, and strategic wisdom they knew was within their abilities.

I began to wonder if the program of mindfulness practice I had been following might be used to cultivate some of the innate capabilities of the mind directly related to leading with excellence. It had already had an impact on my own life that went way beyond stress reduction. It was transforming the way I met the chaos of life, and this change was starting to be noticed and felt by others.

One late afternoon I was sitting at my desk. I looked at my watch and noticed that it was time to go home. I also noticed feeling a sense of satisfaction and completion about the day's work. Almost immediately, I could remember the hundreds of days when that was not the case. I would look at my watch and be shocked that it was time to go home already, and I would wonder where the day went.

This little moment was a breakthrough. It told me a great deal about how much things were changing for me as a result of mindfulness training. Although I am still far from being able to be mindful all the time, the change has been the difference between being here for my family and my work, and missing my life.

SHARING MY DISCOVERIES WITH MY COLLEAGUES

It was the fall of 2005, and I found myself walking with a friend to an officers' meeting. The topic was innovation. We had set aside an entire afternoon to talk about what hindered the creative process and what fostered it. We were exploring all possible methods for encouraging more new ideas that broke fresh ground.

We sat at small tables and worked with a facilitator to try to identify the hurdles that stood in the way of greater innovation. After we had met for hours and made little progress, one vice president stood up and, sounding a bit frustrated, said, "Look, it isn't that we don't have great ideas. We do. We have smart, creative people. But here's what happens when someone offers a team a new idea. Everyone sitting around the table jumps on it at once with comments like 'We have no money for that, the exec wing will never buy it, something similar was done ten years ago, it will take too long,' and so on and so on. Before the idea even takes a breath to see if there might be something there, it's dead." His words rang true to the group.

I knew at that moment that I had to begin to find a way to bring mindfulness training to the process of cultivating leadership excellence. What I heard that vice president describe was the way the mind tells stories and the way those stories often limit us, individually and organizationally. Now the challenge would be to develop a training that would be acceptable to a rather conservative organization with leaders who were already considered very well trained.

To have the greatest organizational impact in the shortest amount of time, I would have to make my initial approach at the level of officers and directors. I had been an officer at General Mills for some time by then and knew this group of professionals to be bright and dedicated and always in search of excellence. I also knew that we all had access to a wide variety of the latest and best leadership training, so mindful leadership training would have to cross a very high bar.

Because I had begun to use the practice specifically to help me improve my effectiveness as a leader, to take on greater responsibilities, to connect more deeply with the people in my life, and to still maintain some equilibrium, I was not interested in bringing in the training as a stress-reduction/health-improvement program. This training of the mind would be about finding a different way to lead, a way that would first support the leader and then have a broader impact on the organization at large, and eventually the community.

I began to have individual conversations with some of my colleagues, sharing my experience and inviting them to explore for themselves a new training that Saki and I had developed. When I had fourteen willing participants, Saki and I traveled with them to a small bed-and-breakfast in Minnesota for the first four-day mindful leadership retreat. This retreat would become known as Cultivating Leadership Presence Through Mindfulness. It was an intensive and unique experience, and I was eager to get candid feedback from the participants. I was also a little apprehensive. How were people really feeling about it? I had been in an executive position too long to take success for granted. I wanted to try to measure it and learn more about the nature of the success or failure.

I sent out a simple survey with five open-ended questions:

Was the retreat of value?
Were there parts that were not of value?
What surprised you?
Is the training of value to the organization?
If so, how?

When the surveys were returned, the single most commonly used word was *transformative*.

That response was unprompted, and when colleagues asked the returning participants about their experience, their answer was often just "You need to go." The viral spread began, spawning weekly meditation sessions, bimonthly extended practice sessions, and eventually an annual retreat for alumni. This was never an official company program. It was started and spread by the leaders themselves, and it was the leaders themselves who would soon ask me for a way to train all levels of the divisions they led. This request led to the development of a seven-week class called Mindful Leadership and Wellness. A few years later, I was asked about a training for new managers, which led to a two-day program called Leading Differently: The Power of a Purposeful Pause.

The fact that this training spread virally and that leaders asked for so much additional mindfulness training to support them—and then made the training available for all the employees in their division—is itself a testament to the effectiveness of mindful leadership. As they began to use the mind training to cultivate focus, creativity, clarity, and compassion, the leaders at General Mills found the space to bring greater inspiration and caring into the workplace, and they made sure that others in their charge had access to the training. Seven years later, the journey continues, with more than five hundred employees already trained in mindful leadership and wellness.

In 2008, Saki and I decided to offer this training to leaders from around the world. Once again I began to reach out to leaders individually, this time outside of General Mills. The General Mills alumni did so as well.

The demand for the four-day retreats grew until it became apparent to Saki and me that the mindful leadership work would need its own nonprofit organization and specially trained instructors—instructors who understood what it was like to be in leadership roles and who had developed their own mindfulness practices. With the help, support, and generous encouragement of my family and the many leaders who had experienced the training, I founded the Institute for Mindful Leadership in 2010. The Institute is dedicated to inviting others to embrace mindful leadership training as the missing piece in the development of leadership excellence, accessible to leaders in all sectors of our society and at all levels of an organization. It certainly never was a part of my career plan to leave the practice of law and dedicate myself to the development and instruction of mindful leadership training. The spread of mindful leadership has been an unfolding I could never have imagined, and, in fact, there are still many days when I find myself wondering just exactly how this happened. It is a great privilege to be on this journey, and to help people discover the innate capacities of the mind. I believe mindful leadership training, along with other forms of mindfulness training, has the potential to make a real difference in the lives of individuals, in our organizations, and in our world.

The best chance we have to address many of the world's major issues successfully is to find ways to cultivate some mental space. When leaders make choices that are harmful to an organization, its employees, or the community, it's not due to a lack of IQ: most often, it's a result of an overtaxed schedule and an autopilot existence that leads to careless or reactive decisions. It is also important that those in leadership roles help employees at all levels begin to understand that they, too, have the capacity to lead, to influence others and make clear decisions by being more aware of each moment in the day. As Parker Palmer once wrote, "A leader is a person who has an unusual degree of power to project on other people his or her shadow, or his or her light." We all have the potential to embody that "unusual degree of power." So, what kind of leader are you? Are you projecting shadow or light?

CHAPTER 3

Mindfulness and Leadership Excellence

Leadership is not about titles, positions, or flowcharts. It is about one life influencing another.

JOHN C. MAXWELL

AT THE BEGINNING OF A weekly mindful leadership practice session, David, a newly minted vice president of a large corporation, shared with the rest of the participants his first lesson about the importance of being aware of your actions as a leader.

> I was heading to my office one morning when I ran into a couple of the engineers working in my division. While riding the elevator, we shared some comments about the wintry weather, and I mentioned that I had just been enjoying a lively debate on the radio about a potential method to reduce fuel consumption. They got off the elevator on their floor, and I thought nothing more about it. To my surprise, three weeks later the manager of those engineers proudly presented me with a detailed analysis of the issues being raised by the experts on the radio and the potential costs and benefits to our business. I was so embarrassed! I had just been making conversation. I had no intention for them to spend any time or resources

looking into the matter. The analysis clearly took them away from more pressing and important work.

David got to see the ripple effect that leaders have, for better or worse. The impact of that elevator communication was unintentional and relatively harmless, but it is always useful to remember that everything we do, or fail to do, has an impact on others. This is true for everyone. And as leaders, we have an even greater potential impact. When we're not fully using all of our capabilities, or we're only partially paying attention to what's going on, the chances of a mindless mistake, or a missed opportunity, increase. The news is filled with examples of mindless leadership: intentional and unintentional actions that cause harm.

Haven't we all, in fact, experienced how a seemingly small thoughtless act or omission can have a disproportionate impact? A remark you made in passing three years ago had a big impact on a friend's self-esteem. A question you asked a subordinate in an irritated tone of voice made him feel inadequate, nagged at him for weeks, and became a topic of lunchroom gossip.

We clearly need to be aware of how even small actions can ripple outward, causing harm or great benefit. How do we cultivate our ability to lead more mindfully, to lead with excellence, by making the most of the fact that the effects of our action can ripple way beyond our immediate sphere?

Let's begin to answer that question with a brief reflection on what we mean by leadership excellence.

(To access a guided audio version of the meditation below and other practices in this book, go to the website (www.Findingthe SpacetoLead.com), where you can listen to or download the audio recordings. In the text, the symbol ▶ indicates an accompanying recording.)

REFLECTION ON LEADERSHIP EXCELLENCE

> ▶ Begin by sitting comfortably and closing your eyes. Notice the sensations of your breath. Allow your mind to let go of distractions.
>
> When you're ready, bring to mind a person you believe embodies leadership excellence. This could be someone you know personally or a leader you have read about.
>
> Allowing yourself some time to let the answers arise, ask yourself the following questions:
>
> Why did this person come to mind?
> What is it about this person's leadership that made you think of him or her when asked about leadership excellence?
>
> Be patient; hold the question in your mind with a sense of openness and curiosity. You don't need to overthink the question.
> Set aside the first answer or two to see if more qualities emerge.
> As you open your eyes, you may find it helpful to write your answers on a piece of paper before reading further.

When you listened for your responses to the reflection questions, you might have noticed that they did not include too many of the most common typical measures of organizational leadership. For example, you probably did not put *consistently makes his quarterly numbers* as the reason you admire the person as someone who leads with excellence. Rather, your list might have included some of the qualities named by other leaders who have explored this reflection with me:

Respectful
Open thinker

Compassionate
Clear vision
Able to inspire
Great listener
Creative
Patient
Collaborative
Kind
Teacher

It's not that hitting the quarterly numbers isn't important; it is. However, what sets people apart as leaders is something much bigger than quantitative metrics. In the work I have done as a corporate officer, and in the work I have done teaching mindful leadership, I have found that the qualities mentioned in response to this reflection come from deep personal experiences. The people we call to mind in this reflection have touched us, inspired us, and made us feel their leadership. The qualities can be rolled up into just two capacities of leadership excellence, and these two capacities are embodied by those we identify as leading with excellence.

First is the *ability of a leader to connect*—to self, to others, and to the larger community.

Connecting to *self* is how we stay connected to our values and our ethics. It's the rudder we steer with in the midst of the chaos.

How deeply we are able to connect authentically with *others* is the difference between an organizational environment that values inclusion and one that is insular and divided into silos that rarely communicate with each other. It's that inclusion that sets the tone for a workplace that is respectful and collaborative.

Finally, connecting to the *community* comes from
being able to see the bigger picture and not get
caught up in the minutiae of a single objective. That
wider connection is how great organizations give
meaning to their existence and inspire their employees.
In the example of the chocolate recall in Chapter 1, the
ability of the leaders to stay connected to themselves,
each other, and their consumers helped them find the
right choice.

Second is the *ability of a leader to skillfully initiate or guide
change*. The important word is *skillfully*—leading not by command and control but by collaborating and listening with open
curiosity and a willingness, at times, to live within ambiguity
until a decision becomes clear. It's also this capacity that fuels a
leader's willingness to take a courageous stand, lead the organization or industry into new arenas, and accept failures as experi-
ments from which to learn.

If we look more deeply into these two capacities, we can find
four fundamentals of leadership excellence: focus, clarity, creativity, and compassion. While you might think of other behaviors or
characteristics that great leaders exhibit, in my experience, these
four are the "must haves," and when one or more of them is lacking, your ability to connect, or your ability to skillfully initiate or
guide change, is significantly impeded.

THE FUNDAMENTALS OF LEADERSHIP EXCELLENCE

These four fundamentals of leadership excellence—*focus, clarity,
creativity*, and *compassion*—are qualities that originate within
our minds and hearts, and we can strengthen and cultivate them
through mindful leadership training. Let's consider each of them
in turn.

FOCUS

COMPASSION — LEADERSHIP EXCELLENCE — CREATIVITY

CLARITY

Focus

More and more often, I hear about the struggles people have maintaining focus. In the workplace and in business schools, people are noticing their difficulties in sustaining attention. I was talking with a leading business school professor recently who was asking about the possibility of getting mindful leadership training for his students, because they were finding it so difficult to get through the demanding reading schedule. Perhaps you've noticed that you need to more frequently reread documents, or that it takes much longer to get through a document than you had anticipated. It's difficult to stay focused on an article or a project, or even a conversation. Too often, even when we intend to stay fully attentive, we notice our thoughts wandering away, distracted by virtually anything that pops up, including our own thinking.

What are the ramifications of this shaky focus?

When you're distracted, you lose productivity. For example, you set aside an hour to sit down and write a report on a recent project. Pretty soon, however, your mind gets distracted by the bell that signals an incoming text or e-mail. You can't help but turn your attention to reading it, and pretty soon five minutes have passed as you write a quick response or just check in with Facebook or

LinkedIn to see what's new. To make matters worse, when you finally return to the report, you need to spend time getting your mind back to where you left off, returning to some of the background you had already read just to get warmed up again. This reset takes time, and it interrupts the stream of steady focus needed to delve deeply into complex strategic issues and potential opportunities.

Another loss of productivity occurs when your focus wanes in a conversation or meeting. When this happens, you also lose connectivity. The connections you form when you're fully present—and therefore fully listening—can make the difference between someone you are leading leaving an encounter feeling heard or leaving an encounter feeling disrespected.

You might wonder if people can tell if your mind is wandering when they're speaking to you. Can they notice when your focus wanes and your mind wanders to the next meeting if you maintain eye contact and nod your head from time to time? Of course they know. Just think back to a time when you had something important to say to your manager and you sat across the desk from her as you spoke. She looked straight at you and occasionally nodded her head and smiled, and yet, as you left her office, you had the unmistakable sense that she wasn't really listening. How did you know? You knew because the kind of focus that brings our attention fully to what's being said is a connection the speaker can sense. When your mind wanders for a significant period of time, the connection is lost.

If you begin working with the practices in mindful leadership designed to strengthen your focus, you can learn how to notice when your mind wanders away from the present moment and learn how to work with the wandering mind by redirecting your attention back to the present. Over time, you notice the wandering mind more and more quickly. You build the mind's capacity to aim and sustain focus. This develops your ability to connect with others, and it develops your ability to bring your full concentration to issues and opportunities.

Clarity

In the constant busy-ness of business, you may often find yourself moving from one subject to another so quickly that you don't clearly see what's in front of you. You see only what you expect to see, what you hope to see, or what you want to see.

So often, we do not use our innate capability to challenge our own assumptions and to see what is actually here!

Gordon MacKenzie, the author of *Orbiting the Giant Hairball* and an innovation pioneer from within Hallmark, explained this kind of blindness as believing in a model:

> The more fully we believe a model is reality, the more rigid the model becomes. And the more rigid it becomes, the more it confines us. There is a sense of security in this, the sense of security that comes from being contained by the "known" and thus shielded from the threat of the unknown. So the mixed blessing of models is that while they can generate a sense of coherence through a groundedness (in "knowledge"), they can also, if used without mindfulness, become addicting anesthetics to the pain of an inscrutable universe and further insulate us from full reality, which is the realm of infinite possibilities.

Learning to stop long enough to notice when you are stuck in a model, or when you are in reactivity mode, is a part of mindful leadership training that develops our ability to see clearly what is here—the issues and the opportunities—and to *choose* how to respond, which may mean challenging the model. Sometimes, the clarity will help us decide that the right response to a situation right now is to do nothing, because there are times when, despite our bias for action, the wisest decision is to wait and see what develops.

Cultivating our ability to develop greater clarity applies not only to seeing clearly the events and environment around us, but also to seeing ourselves more clearly. As we begin to notice, for example, our own reactivity to certain situations, and the various ways in which our conditioning and education may be filtering out some of what we need to see, we often make important discoveries. Those discoveries can often lead us to make important changes.

Kevin was a successful entrepreneur. As he developed his mindful leadership practice, he began to see, he said, "how my view of myself was impacting my leadership. When I was feeling as though I was falling short of my own expectations, I thought everyone around me was falling short of my expectations. When I could finally see how these thoughts were affecting my leadership, their grip on me began to soften, and I began to change." In the process of noticing his criticism of himself and questioning its value, Kevin was also able to see those times when his negative feedback to others was unwarranted and hurtful.

As the world continues to shrink, markets become more global, and resources become more scarce, the old playbook no longer applies. We need leaders with the ability to see clearly what is here, not an imagined or historical version of what is here. Then the best choices about how to proceed can be made. We need leaders who are aware of their own filters and conditioning. We need them to notice the critical voice in their head, their fears of the unknown, their discomfort with risks, their fear of failure, and their propensity to seek the safety of old models. In the process of this self-examination, leaders find their authenticity and their ability to skillfully work with colleagues to effect change. To reach our goal of leading with courage and integrity, we need a new playbook based on the ability to see the environment of today.

Creativity

As William Duggan of the Columbia Business School points out in his books *Strategic Intuition* and *Creative Strategy*, flashes of insight are a core element in innovation, and recent brain science has taught us that creativity requires some slow time for the brain and that "presence of mind gives you better ideas." Similarly, as she writes in *Red Thread Thinking*, Debra Kaye's research told her that we need to remove ourselves periodically from "task-based focus" so we have a time when we can stumble upon a new connection or association. The creative brain craves that space. But when we have a calendar fully packed with meetings, and a task list that fills several pages, the spaciousness we require for creativity is minimal.

Creative solutions and ideas have a better chance of arising when the mind is not constantly busy with to-do lists. Have you ever noticed that setting up a deadline for generating a creative solution is not nearly as fruitful as creating some additional spaciousness in the day, time to let the mind be creative? How many times have you awakened in the morning with an answer to a problem, or perhaps had it pop into your head while you were in the shower? The mind needs some time to pull away from all the analytical thinking for the creative and innovative solutions to emerge.

Why?

A constant stream of thinking actually gets in the way of wisdom that lies deep within each of us, what we have learned and experienced over time and stored because of its importance. When we're racing around, this valuable resource we've developed and inherited is lost to us. It gets buried in the distractions of the present.

The good news is that you can train your mind to stand in a different relationship to the constant stream of thoughts. In the process, you can leave more space for creativity.

Compassion

Compassion arises from our understanding of suffering and our desire to alleviate that suffering. Empathy, which connects us with other people's feelings, is sometimes used as a synonym for compassion, but in my understanding and experience genuine compassion goes beyond empathy. Our compassionate mind recognizes that our empathy arises from the understanding that we all share a common humanity. Compassion reminds us that when we see someone suffering, we are separated from the sufferer by only the thinnest lines of time and circumstance, and we feel a pull to lessen the suffering.

As we cultivate our innate ability to be compassionate, we also see that we may have been turning away from suffering even when we had the ability to relieve it in some way. That turning away often includes turning away from seeing how we may actually be creating suffering, for others and for ourselves. How many parents have failed to notice the pain that a judgmental remark may create for a teenager? It's hard to alleviate that suffering when you don't even see that you are the cause of it.

Cultivating compassion begins with self-compassion. When we engage in self-compassion, we are willing to make room in our lives to see our own suffering and to offer ourselves some kindness.

This was not an easy lesson for me to learn, and it is not an easy lesson for most leaders. In the twenty-five years I have held leadership positions, I've had the great privilege of working with wonderful people in all sectors of our society. They were leaders working incredibly hard with interminable lists of obligations and responsibilities, and they generally put themselves at the bottom of the list. We don't think we need compassion. It may even feel selfish or self-indulgent. Everyone needs compassion, though, whether it is obvious to a passerby or not—and like other qualities associated with the best of humanity, such as love and happiness, compassion cannot truly be offered to others until we first offer it to ourselves. It is an integral part of knowing ourselves more deeply and opening our heart more fully.

Compassion helps us to understand ourselves and others, and the overwhelming similarities we all share. It helps us to understand the interconnections among us. It encourages us to become involved with the well-being of those around us. This fundamental of leadership excellence is often an important element in creating a plan to make a difference with the work that we do, or to make important changes in how we do our work. It reminds us that the best leaders work in the service of others while also caring for their own well-being. Compassion is a powerful guiding force for great leaders, yet it is often misunderstood, and consequently greatly undervalued or excluded from our workplaces. What a missed opportunity.

JUST AS WE know that we can develop the *body's* innate capacities to increase our strength, flexibility, and resiliency, we now know from neuroscience that we can develop the *mind's* innate capacities—including its capacity to focus, see clearly, be creative, and act with compassion. In the coming chapters, you will see how you can develop a simple *daily meditation practice* and add *purposeful pauses* throughout your day that will begin to train your mind to cultivate and strengthen each of these capacities.

We can no longer afford to have people in positions of influence lead without using their minds to full capacity. They need the tools and training to counteract the effects of 24/7 connectivity, multitasking, and information overload. We need the kind of leadership excellence that more consistently finds a win-win-win—good for the organization, good for the employees, good for the community.

Organizations in many industries are beginning to find those win-win-win scenarios. Rather than marketing campaigns that just sell more products through a contest or other promotion, we see marketing campaigns that encourage consumers to buy products and, in return, the selling organization shares some portion of the proceeds with a nonprofit entity such as the American Heart Association, the Nature Conservancy, or the Special Olympics. These campaigns are good for business, inspire the employees, and help the nonprofit organizations: win-win-win.

We are beginning to see organizations look to more sustainable manufacturing and packaging. Those organizations understand the ripple effect and realize that the earth's finite resources must be carefully managed if human beings are going to survive. They have discovered that many times the changes they make to protect our environment are also good for business. More and more, consumers are drawn to the products produced by organizations with an appreciation for the stewardship responsibility leadership brings.

But these changes are just the beginning—these actions are still in the minority. There is much more that needs to be done, and the challenge to find these innovative solutions is often very attractive to good leaders when they have some space to attend to the possibilities. Cultivating more space through mindful leadership practices and applications may increase the number and scope of projects like these, as well as many other as yet undiscovered win-win-win scenarios.

We need more people who can lead with excellence—focused, clear-seeing, creative, and compassionate. We need people who are connected to themselves, those around them, and the community. We need leaders who know how to skillfully initiate change. We need men and women who embody leadership presence.

Fortunately, our leaders—and all of us—are born with all the raw materials we need. The capability to be present is innate; it just needs training. In the Institute retreats and workshops that my colleagues and I teach to employees and leaders from around the world, we repeatedly hear people say that this experience and practice allows them to see a fuller and more meaningful way to meet the realities of their lives.

Mike, a physician from Massachusetts, described his experience this way:

> What's unique about leadership training that employs mindfulness is that it doesn't ask me to be different. It invites me to be more of who I already am.

As a leader, your best hope for influencing in an innovative and authentic way begins with becoming fully aware of who you are, and then seeing clearly what is around you. When you are able to do that, when you are able to change your relationship to your world in this dynamic way, there's no limit to the potential positive impact you can have. Your actions, be they ever so small, can move mountains.

PART 2

Meditation Practices for Leaders

CHAPTER 4

Cushions, Clearing the Mind, and Other Myths

To pay attention, this is our endless and proper work.
MARY OLIVER

IF YOU GOOGLE MINDFULNESS MEDITATION, within the millions of hits you'll find a mind-boggling stream of definitions and a plethora of techniques for learning about mindfulness. So, what exactly is mindfulness training in the context of *Finding the Space to Lead*?

Since there is a lot of misunderstanding about meditation and mindfulness, let's start by listing what we're not talking about.

Mindfulness training is not:

A religion
A technique for clearing away thoughts
A new age method involving chanting or incense
A relaxation technique
A training in deep breathing
A way to *eliminate* stress

Mindfulness training *is* a method of developing the mind's innate capabilities, including the capabilities that are most directly involved in the development of leadership excellence (as we saw in

Chapter 3). The beauty of mindfulness training is that the techniques are simple (which does not mean *easy*) and require no special equipment to carry out.

BASIC MINDFULNESS MEDITATION INSTRUCTIONS

▶ 1. Find a comfortable seated position, allowing your body to become still and feel supported. A straight-back chair works just fine. Meditation cushions are not needed, although you can certainly choose to use them. Sitting on a meditation cushion does not make you a better meditator. If you want to sit on the floor, I offer instructions for that in "Tips for Daily Meditation" on page 49.

2. Choose to bring your attention to a specific object. Any object can be the focus for mindfulness meditation, but in the beginning, it is most helpful to focus your attention on something that your senses will easily notice, such as your breath or the sounds around you. (In later chapters, we will discuss focusing your attention on thoughts and emotions.)

3. As you intentionally direct your attention, bring an open curiosity to whatever you notice. You do not need to change or control or assess what you are noticing.

4. Notice when your attention is pulled away or drifts away, and redirect your attention back to the object. There is no need to judge how well you are doing with the practice.

Let's take a specific example to illustrate a mindfulness meditation you can try right now.

Choose a place to sit that feels comfortable.

Bring your attention to the sensations you notice as the breath enters and leaves the body.

Whether you feel the breath most strongly at the nostrils, in the chest, or deep in the belly, aim and sustain your attention on the sensations of the entire in-breath and the entire out-breath in that area of the body.

When you notice your mind has drifted off—for example, running through your to-do list, rehearsing what you're going to say to someone, or playing a little movie in your head—redirect your attention back to the sensations of the breath. There is no need to change your normal breath and no need for deep breathing exercises. Just notice the sensations that are already available to notice. There is nothing to change, control, or fix. Just be aware of the way the body experiences each in-breath and each out-breath.

Sounds pretty simple, right? Try this first practice for about ten minutes.

If you're like most of us, this little exercise can be a bit surprising. Even if you formed a strong intention to simply pay attention to the sensations you were noticing, for example, in your chest as the ribs expanded with the in-breath and released with the out-breath, pretty soon your mind became distracted by a thought about dinner tonight, or a sound in the room, or a discomfort somewhere in your body.

What went wrong?

Nothing!

You had an opportunity to notice the flitting nature of the mind. Even when we want to aim and sustain our attention on the sensations of the breath, we often find we need to keep redirecting our focus. In today's world, the mind is constantly pulled in different directions, so it has been conditioned to jump around. We almost never fully attend to anything anymore. We live in a state of continuous partial attention. A practice that trains our singular focus is a bit foreign to us.

The problem with the flitting nature of our minds is that when we need to stay focused on a difficult issue or conversation, we often find that it's nearly impossible to do so for any length of time. Most of us have not been offered the training necessary to build our concentration, but we can all avail ourselves of this simple-to-understand technique that begins to cultivate and strengthen our innate capability to sustain attention.

Although the fundamental framework is simple, the actual practice requires discipline and self-compassion: the discipline to consistently redirect your wandering mind back to the object of attention, and an equal amount of self-compassion to redirect your attention gently and without judgment.

Doing so can be especially difficult when you're used to the intense self-judgment often trained into those who are driven to achieve. Try to let go of the judging and simply notice when your mind has wandered off the object, then redirect your attention. I once heard a meditation teacher describe the approach as analogous to training a puppy to listen. When the puppy's attention is distracted from the learning at hand, you gently and firmly bring it back to the training. There is something playful and light about this analogy that I have always liked. We would be patient and kind to a puppy even as we continue to teach it. Why should we offer ourselves anything less kind?

This is the first daily meditation practice. Make time twice each day to practice for ten minutes. This basic meditation will be an important building block as you move into specific mindful leadership trainings that ask you to aim and sustain attention as a way to create space in your day and to begin to explore bringing the practice into many different parts of your daily life. All the practices invite you to be in the present moment, a necessity if you are to cultivate leadership presence.

Mindfulness meditation practice requires regularity and repetition to work. Just as regular exercise develops your body's innate capacity to be strong, flexible, and resilient, a daily meditation practice develops your mind's ability to be more resilient, responsive, and clear. Now, before your thoughts turn to "I can't possibly add one more thing to my schedule," ask yourself if there are ten minutes in your morning, and ten more at another time during the day, that you spend on something less useful than developing your mind. Can you drop something to make room for a daily meditation practice? If you're like most high-achieving leaders I've known, it might help to remember that when you're cultivating leadership presence through mindfulness, you're not only helping yourself, you're becoming better able to help others.

TIPS FOR DAILY MEDITATION

1. A daily meditation practice of ten minutes twice a day, every day, is much better than only an hour of practice on Saturday. Consistency is important.
2. If you find sitting still for ten minutes too difficult, try taking a walk or engaging in some other form of exercise before beginning to practice.
3. If you are sitting on a chair, sit with your feet flat on the floor, your back, neck, and head straight, and your hands placed comfortably in your lap.
4. If you want to sit on the floor, you can fold up a blanket and place a pillow or two on it, or you can use a meditation cushion. Cross your legs in front of you and sit on the front half of the cushion, slightly tipping your pelvis forward so that your knees more easily move toward resting on the floor. Place your hands comfortably on your legs. (If this posture creates discomfort, move to the chair! Remember: Using a meditation cushion does not make you a better meditator.)

5. If you miss a day, or a few days, just begin again. The daily meditation practice is as close to you as the next ten minutes.

During a recent mindful leadership retreat, Maria, a midcareer engineer, audibly sighed at the end of a late-afternoon practice session. When I asked if there was anything she wanted to say, she replied that she was feeling frustrated because she just didn't think she was getting the hang of this meditation. She went on to explain that in the early-morning practice session she was able to sustain attention on her breath for long periods of time, redirecting her attention only occasionally. But that afternoon when she was practicing, she noticed her mind was constantly distracted away from the breath, and she was having a "terrible" time. Her attention was being pulled away by thoughts of her family, thoughts of a new assignment she was worrying about, and sometimes just by the sound of the other participants coughing in the room.

I reminded her that the instructions for mindfulness meditation practice include noticing when the mind is distracted and then simply redirecting it back to the object of attention—in this case, the sensations of the breath. I asked her if that was what she was practicing. She paused for a moment and then said, "Yes, but I thought this session would be like the session this morning when my mind had fewer thoughts pulling it away. I really liked that spacious feeling. I wanted to get back to that."

Maria's frustration had its roots in creating expectations about what the experience should be like, which can sabotage our intention to develop a daily meditation practice. What Maria concluded was a "terrible" meditation was simply the activity level of her mind in that moment. There was nothing terrible about her practice. She assumed the meditation practice would be the same each time. It's not. You're training the mind to notice when the attention wanders and redirect it. The redirection is the practice. This is how you begin to train the mind to sustain attention at other times of the day when you're not engaged in the daily meditation practice. Instead of accepting that there is nothing you can do about your mind's propensity to daydream or to think about home while at work, or about work while at home, you learn to notice when you are physically in one place and mentally in another. Most importantly, you learn how to redirect your attention back to the present moment. The flitting mind that we notice during our practice sessions is the same active mind that is with each of us all day long. With mindfulness practice, you can begin to strengthen your capacity to pay attention and begin to learn more about what it means to be present.

DESK CHAIR MEDITATION

Most of us spend a great deal of time sitting behind our desks. For the fifteen years that I was a corporate officer at General Mills, I certainly spent much of my day sitting in a chair, in my office, conference rooms, colleagues' offices. It seemed natural, then, to develop a meditation practice that people could use while sitting at work.

If you can find ten minutes in a relatively quiet place during the workday, the desk chair meditation can become one of your two ten-minute practices for each day. You may need to be creative to find the quiet place. Many participants have told me that they're best able to do this practice by first leaving their office and finding an empty conference room, or even leaving the building to sit in their car during part of their lunch break. The desk chair part of the title for the desk chair meditation need not be taken literally. This meditation can be done anywhere you are able to sit quietly and practice, even an airplane seat.

> ▶ Begin the desk chair meditation by bringing your attention
> to the sensations of your breath. When you're ready, direct
> your attention to the soles of your feet, opening your mind to what-
> ever sensations are there to be noticed. Perhaps you are noticing the
> pressure on the soles of your feet as the weight of your legs rests on
> them. Perhaps the soles of your feet feel warm or cool. Just notice.
> No need to judge or engage in discursive thinking. If your mind is
> pulled away or wanders, redirect your attention, firmly and gently.
>
> Move your attention next to the tops of your feet, ankles, lower
> legs, knees, and so forth. Gradually scan through your body, noticing
> sensations, noticing discomfort, and noticing areas of your body
> where you detect an absence of sensations. You simply don't notice
> any sensations in your shoulders right now, for example. No need to
> search for sensations; just keep scanning through your body, taking
> your time and being open to what is here.

This second daily meditation practice is another way to cultivate your ability to pay attention, and it is also valuable for pick-
ing up on important messages from your body that you often
ignore or don't fully understand. These messages fall into two
categories. First, we take in information about our physical well-
being, which we will begin to explore in this chapter. Second, we
take in information about our emotions, which we will explore in
Chapter 12.

When you scan through your body, you notice whatever sensations are there, including areas of the body that feel tight or sore or
painful. You may also notice a more generalized feeling of sleepiness
or illness. For many people, these discoveries are surprising, either
for the very fact of their existence at all, or for the extent to which
they make themselves known. These sensations are the language of
the body, and when you bring attention to them, you can hear what

your body is telling you more clearly. In fact, human beings not only have the capacity to feel sensations using the nerve receptors on the skin, we have the capacity for interoception—sensing the signals sent from the *inside* of the body. If these are hardwired capabilities, why don't we hear these messages more consistently?

There are many possible answers. Perhaps our overscheduled, nonstop existence leaves no space for the attention required to care well for ourselves. Or maybe a penchant for doing things perfectly leaves little time for being sick. Many of us were trained to always play hurt and sublimate pain as we strove for excellence. Whatever the reason, when I ask groups of leaders how many have noticed that they only get sick on the weekends or on vacation, the room becomes a sea of raised hands. Why is that? Perhaps in that small amount of downtime, the messages of the body that were drowned out during the week had a chance to be heard. If we stop for a moment to consider this scenario, we realize that when the sensations are ignored for too long, the body may keep turning up the volume until it can't be drowned out, and at that point it can mean a very serious health problem has emerged.

The desk chair meditation is a way for you to drop in on your body's messages and listen. With the information gathered, you might make some simple choices to care for yourself—doing a few more stretches to alleviate a sore back, modifying your sleep patterns to influence an ever-present fatigue, adjusting your diet to turn down the heat in your stomach. The desk chair meditation is a ten-minute checkup, or better yet, a ten-minute check-in.

CREATING A PERSONALIZED DAILY MEDITATION PRACTICE

Look at your calendar right now and write in the two times you will practice tomorrow. There is no need to look at this as something you need to fit in for the rest of your life. Just make the time (two ten-minute sessions) to practice tomorrow. One day at a time is the best approach to getting started. Choose to practice with your breath, with sounds, or with the desk chair meditation. Any combination will work fine. If it's more comfortable for you to practice with the breath every time, that is fine. If you like to mix up the practice so that one meditation practice is the breath, the next one is the body scan, that's fine. Create a daily practice that works for you.

Be gentle with your practice. You are beginning a new training. Just like beginning a new exercise regime for your body, introducing a new regimen for your mind takes commitment and discipline, and there will be times when you simply need to choose to begin again. Be courageous and enjoy the discoveries you will begin to make about your mind and its many capabilities.

CHAPTER 5

A Purposeful Pause

Nature's music is never over; her silences are pauses, not conclusions.

MARY WEBB

IF YOU'RE LIKE MOST OF US, YOU can become so accustomed to constant busy-ness—going through the motions of meetings, calls, and conversations—that you are only partly attentive most of the time, and completely inattentive some of the time.

We have a national—if not worldwide—epidemic of continuous partial attention. We go on autopilot for much, or all, of our lives. We begin to believe that this is just how it has to be in the fast-paced, distraction-filled world we work and live in. If we don't live on this incessant treadmill, we'll fall behind, or fail.

What is the cost of this treadmill—personally and professionally? The media carry almost daily reports of a growing body of science that is documenting the physiological and psychological tolls of our modern habit of living under the gun. For our purposes here, though, we need only investigate our own experiences, and the experiences of those around us, to know that the toll is significant. How many people in your own circle take sleeping pills? Antidepressants? Use drinking, or use some other addictive behavior like shopping, eating, or working to excess in an attempt to combat the symptoms? And how often do we wonder how we could have missed an important fact or made such an insensitive remark? We know we are capable of meeting life in a more attentive and compassionate way, but we may believe it is not possible in the speed and complexity of today.

For many years, I collected before-and-after survey data from employees at all levels who were registered to take a seven-week Mindful Leadership and Wellness course. The questions asked about work performance and included one that asked the participant to rate how often "It seems I am running on automatic, without much awareness of what I am doing." Astonishingly, nearly 60 percent of participants reported that they were in this condition frequently.

As managers of organizations, if we were to assume that the employees responding to these surveys were fairly typical, what actions should we take? Have we now created a workforce that is so used to being on autopilot that professionalism, quality, creativity, productivity, and basic human decency are at risk? How often are ethical lapses the result of failing to be fully present to see with clarity the potential impact of our choices?

What about your own workday? How often do you feel as though you could have done more, or better, if only you had some space to breathe? Do you notice this feeling even when you get the job done and others are happy with the results? Is this feeling sometimes related more to how the results were achieved than to what results were achieved?

As noted in Chapter 1, when I've asked leaders what the one thing is they wish they had in greater abundance, it isn't resources or power.

It is *space*.

We need more open spaces so we can step off the treadmill and focus on what is important instead of being pulled along by the demands of the squeaky wheel. We need more space to take the time to celebrate a creative response by the team. We need more space to support the people we are charged with developing. We need more space to listen to our own wisdom.

To counteract this gnawing feeling of needing space and time, you need to find ways to create it. Your life is not likely to lose its complexity anytime soon, and you don't need your life to become less complex in order to make moments of space in your day. You can create those moments of space by regularly taking what I refer to as a *purposeful pause*.

WHAT IS A PURPOSEFUL PAUSE?

It's a moment in the day when you notice the swirl and choose to intentionally pay attention. For example, you notice that you are sitting in a meeting but your mind is speeding into the future or caught in replays of the past—barely noticing what people are saying. At these times, you can use a simple practice to bring your attention back into the room: all it takes is a few moments to intentionally guide your attention back to the present by feeling the breath, hearing the sounds in your surroundings, or noticing the sensations in your body. There is no need to close your eyes or sit in a meditation posture. Just take a purposeful pause.

As you take this purposeful pause, you might notice the settling of your busy mind. Why? Because your mind has returned to the present and let go of the thoughts that were crowding out your capacity to be in the moment. The sensations of the breath, other sensations in the body, and sounds can only be noticed in the present. You can't feel sensations in the future or in the past. You can't hear the sound of the voices from the last meeting, nor the sound of your commuter train whistle later in the day. The sensations you notice in your chest as your ribs expand with the breath can only be felt right now, with the breath of this moment. When you intentionally bring your attention to sensations and sounds, you become more awake to what is all around you and what you feel inside yourself. When the distractions of the past and present are lessened, you can see more clearly what is here in this moment and then choose what to pursue next with greater awareness.

A purposeful pause is available to you at any moment. It's as close as the sensations of the next breath in your body, or the sensations of your feet on the floor. You don't need to find a quiet room or a meditation cushion. Wherever you are—in the midst of whatever meeting or call, or even as you are walking to your next appointment—intentionally escorting your attention to the sensations in the body is a powerful way to interrupt the discursive mind, and to calm the racing pulse or release the tightness in the throat that may arise as part of the body's reactions to thoughts of the future or the past. When you interrupt the treadmill, even for a few moments of practice in this way, your body and mind have a chance to reset, to allow you to see things more clearly, so that you can respond rather than react, and pay attention to that gut feeling that's been calling out to you.

One of the greatest pianists of the twentieth century was Arthur Rubinstein. Near the end of his life, the story goes, he granted a young journalist an interview. Because of his frailty, she was asked to keep her questions short. She thought about this interview for some time and eventually decided that what she most wanted to know was the answer to a very simple question.

She asked him, "What is it about your playing that makes the music sound so incredible?"

The maestro's answer came swiftly. "I play the notes no better than many, but the pauses . . . ah, that makes all the difference." From the stillness of a pause, the next moment flows with greater clarity and warmth and inspiration. This is true of music and of leadership.

Your ability to effectively integrate purposeful pauses on a day-to-day basis is directly related to the consistency of your daily formal practice. For example, as you build your familiarity with directing your attention to the breath sensations during your daily meditation practice, you will find it easier to quickly drop in on those sensations as you are waiting to make a presentation. As you learn to consistently punch holes in the autopilot quality of your day with these purposeful pauses, you will begin to notice how these small moments of mindfulness begin to reshape the next moment.

PUTTING PURPOSEFUL PAUSES TO WORK

A couple of years ago, I had the opportunity to teach daily meditation practice and purposeful pauses to an entire corporate department that had identified fostering innovation as one of its most important priorities. In speaking with members of the department, it became clear that there was a general sentiment that developing a stronger culture of innovation would require department members to have more open time, more space.

They told me they didn't have time for informal conversations, or to debrief or hold postmortems on recently completed projects or do midstream reviews of current projects. They said they didn't have space to listen to their own kernels of ideas and kick them around with a few colleagues. They were constantly going from meeting to meeting, assignment to assignment, and didn't know any other way to go about their work.

Would a mindful leadership approach be helpful?

I didn't know, but I was certainly familiar with the realities of the workplace they were describing, and I had noticed the leadership changes in myself and others as we developed our mindful leadership practices. But what about the specific impact on innovation? The head of the department was motivated to try something different. So the members of the department and I took the leap.

We began with a department meeting where I explained the experiment and introduced the group to a simple daily meditation practice. Although the experience of sitting together in a conference room was familiar to the group, sitting in silence was new. Within a few moments, however, the stillness and silence seemed to envelop the room. This first practice set the stage for the journey to explore new things, starting with mindful leadership training and then moving to the new, innovative processes and ways of working that would hopefully lead to a more innovative environment for the department.

I asked each person to make room in his or her schedule for a ten-minute daily meditation practice. I then moved on to introduce purposeful pauses and asked each person to find two places in the day to integrate a purposeful pause. We created an internal website where the group could capture ideas for purposeful pauses, as well as report on the struggles they were encountering.

A month later, we reconvened to meditate as a group and to talk about what people noticed when they tried to work with their minds in this way, consciously creating pauses and space. First, people spoke about how difficult it was to remember their daily meditation practice and to take purposeful pauses. Habits are difficult to change at first. It requires discipline and intention. They began to notice that they could get carried away with the busy-ness and forget in the heat of the moment. However, they also began to notice that as the days of daily meditation practice increased, the ability to catch themselves when they were in the midst of the swirl increased. As that capacity increased, so did their ability to bring their attention to the present moment by first bringing it to body sensations.

Individuals talked about their discoveries. Some were surprised to notice that they seemed to have a daily headache, or tightness in the upper back. Not surprisingly, they began to wonder why those sensations were there. What might they choose to do differently that could alter the duration of that discomfort or circumvent it altogether?

People also reported beginning to see the routine and mindless way they approached their day, and the impact that the purposeful pause began to have on their ability to ensure that they were fully present for an important conversation they were about to have with a spouse, colleague, close friend, son, or daughter.

One engineer said, "I realized that my young son was talking to my belt buckle, not to me." As a result, he got down on the floor and noticed the difference it made in their connection when they were talking with each other. An experienced manager reported that she noticed that her intention to be a strong supporter of her team was being sabotaged because her mind was only partially attentive to the present moment. She had begun to see that when one of her direct reports would come into her office, her mind was still deeply engrossed in the last e-mail she had sent. So she began to take a few moments before her next meeting to close the screen on her computer and use a purposeful pause to mentally prepare. (She would hear later in a 360-degree feedback report that her team members felt more heard and supported than they had at any time in the past.)

Another suggestion I made to the department members for a purposeful pause was to drive to and from work without distractions like phone calls or music. Simply pay attention to driving: noticing the road, other cars, sounds, the feel of the steering wheel and pedals, the many times your attention drifts away, and so on. When people try this practice, they quite frequently say things like "I never noticed that my car has been making some really funny noises; I better get it checked out" or "I've been driving that route for twenty years and never noticed that at the hour I'm coming to work the sunrise is spectacular." One young parent noticed that in the quiet of the drive, she found a needed transition space that enabled her to arrive home fully present for her family, rather than still listening to voicemails from work, with her mind occupied by new to-do list items for the next day. Taking a pause during the daily commute can be a particularly rich practice. Plus, it gives you an up-close look at what it means to be on autopilot while wielding a 2,000-pound potentially lethal weapon.

From the base of a daily meditation practice and purposeful pauses sprinkled throughout the day, the department took the mindful leadership regimen a step further and began to focus more specifically on fostering innovation. We explored how to open up the space many felt was lacking, the space that might enable them to identify and explore innovative opportunities. I gave each person a notebook to place alongside his or her computer and asked them to block out at least a half hour each week to use as a dedicated open space. During the week, as employees noticed something they wished they had more time to explore, they would jot it down in the notebook. Then, when they reached the blocked-out time in the week, they could return to the notebook and choose to attend to one or more of the items. We named this notebook and the blocked-out time on the calendar after a corner in the Monopoly game, Free Parking.

Did you ever play Monopoly and find that you were really happy when you landed on Free Parking? It was the square where you were able to take a breath, and if you played like my family did, you might also find some surprise riches there from past fines paid in the game. So it seemed like a great name for taking our daily practice and purposeful pauses to the next step.

The variety of items the department members wrote in their Free Parking notebooks ranged from "time to read some research without interruption" to "time to network with an industry specialist" to "time to clear my desk on Friday so I can come into a cleared space on Monday." A number learned that they needed to actually leave their work area during the time blocked out for Free Parking ideas, or that time would simply disappear, swallowed up by the rush of the day.

Others found it useful to coordinate their Free Parking time with colleagues, so they would have time set aside just for exploring a new idea together. The practice of intentionally blocking out open space became a key element in helping the group to see what benefits for innovation can accrue from having some breathing space, rather than just hoping that it will emerge entirely on its own from the maelstrom of the daily work world. The group began to become more adept at seeing the opportunities that might benefit from more space.

People in the group told stories of increased clarity, more innovative ideas, and greater productivity. For example, one director shared the story of trying to identify a new name for an initiative to be instituted in the entire organization in the upcoming year. His team had not come up with an answer in the past six months, and the deadline was fast approaching. Rather than scheduling more meetings for brainstorming sessions, they decided to set aside time to individually reflect on the issue, using the practices they had been learning. In a silent drive, one of the team members came upon the new name. As he later reported to the team, he was surprised that it just arose, not as a result of intensive analytical thinking, but in the spaciousness of allowing the mind to rest in the present moment.

As important as these tangible examples are as evidence of potential direct benefits to the bottom line, the reports about how people responded to working with the mind in this way are equally significant. They spoke about how excited they were at the discovery that there was a training that could show them an alternative way of being with the hustle and bustle of their complicated lives. Mindful leadership training was not requiring them to change their lives, to go more slowly, or to work less. It was cultivating an innate capability that enabled them to be more intentional about how they chose to spend their time.

As they found opportunities to insert purposeful pauses into their days, they began to feel a genuine difference. In small but significant ways, they began the journey of discovering how to live life more fully than they could on autopilot. They had no need to push anything away or drop out of the work they were doing. Rather, they could begin to be aware of what was here, how they were meeting it, and then make an intentional choice about what made sense to do next.

BASIC PURPOSEFUL PAUSE INSTRUCTIONS

Right now, make a list of three places in your day when you will take a purposeful pause. It can be any time in the day or evening when you will intentionally bring attention to what you notice, and redirect your attention when the mind wanders or is pulled away. Until the practices become part of your day, it may be helpful to write them into your calendar, or put a note on your dashboard or bathroom mirror. Some suggestions:

Mindfully brush your teeth. Notice the taste of the toothpaste, the sounds the water makes, the water temperature.

Mindfully drink that first coffee of the day. Smell the aroma. Feel the warmth of the cup. Taste the brew on your tongue.

Mindfully walk from your car to your destination. Feel your body moving the air, your feet on the ground. Hear the sounds of your surroundings.

Mindfully drive to and from work. Just drive, no radio or voicemails. Listen to the sounds around you. Feel the steering wheel, the pedals, the seat cushions, the touch of air on your skin.

Mindfully eat your lunch. Instead of surfing the Web or texting, notice how you're nourishing your body. Pay attention to the colors, smells, textures, and tastes of your food.

Every few weeks, choose an additional place in the day to add a purposeful pause. You may begin to notice an increased sense of calm and greater energy reserves. Finding these moments to pull yourself out of your constant stream of planning for the future and worrying about the past allows you to rest and recharge your body and your mind.

CHAPTER 6

Reduce the Noise,
Capture the Signal

The greatest compliment that was ever paid me was when one asked me what I thought, and attended to my answer.

HENRY DAVID THOREAU

BETH, A SENIOR DIRECTOR OF A large sales organization, returned from several days out of the office to an in-box brimming with requests and a calendar even more packed than normal. She took a few moments with her calendar to see if anything could be eliminated or postponed so she could breathe some air into her day, and her eye was drawn to a mentoring meeting scheduled for later that morning. It would be a challenging meeting, so she considered moving it to give her more time. She was supposed to meet with a midlevel employee, Catherine, whose performance had been deteriorating. The decline seemed based more on Catherine's attitude than on her capability. Catherine was in trouble, and the mentoring program was the last attempt to try to help her job performance improve. If Beth's mentoring wasn't successful, this young woman would be terminated.

Several weeks earlier, Beth had volunteered to take this one last try with Catherine. They scheduled weekly meetings where they would agree on specific assignments for the week and then review them at the next week's meeting. With so much at stake for Catherine, Beth decided it was better to keep to the schedule. She left the meeting on her calendar, rearranged some other obligations, and left her office for her first meeting of the day.

Not surprisingly, Beth's meetings began to run over. When the time came for the meeting with Catherine, Beth was hurrying to return to her office. When she arrived, Catherine was waiting for her. They exchanged greetings, and Beth went right to work by asking Catherine, "So, how did the assignments go?" Catherine's immediate response was to say simply, "I didn't do them" with no hint that she wanted to elaborate.

Beth later told me the reactions she was noticing in her mind and body when she heard Catherine's response. She said, "I could feel the frustration and anger rising right from my toes and coursing through my whole body. I could notice my thoughts go right to the words I typically would have said. Things like 'Don't you care if you get fired? Why are you being irresponsible?' And even 'Don't you know that I had other things to attend to but moved them for this meeting?'"

However, she could also sense that something was going on with her colleague. She took a pause, allowed herself to feel a few breaths in her body, let go of those reactive judgments and questions, and heard herself asking, "Are you okay?" In the next moment, Catherine began to sob, and eventually she was able to recount to Beth the tragic events that had been unfolding in her home life over the past several months. Catherine's husband had been diagnosed with a degenerative neurological disease. The prognosis was dire under the best of circumstances and a few weeks ago, her husband had decided to stop all treatments. In the past week, Catherine found herself giving up as well.

Beth and Catherine made a connection that would not have been possible if Beth had hurried into a typical conversation and fired off her judgmental reactions. She listened to more than just the words, and she cared enough to take the time to ask about

Catherine, not just her assignments. Beth's approach afforded Catherine the security she needed to open up about what was going on.

For Beth, a purposeful pause allowed her to notice the feeling that something important lurked there unsaid. She told me later that after the meeting, she wondered how many times in the past she had not really heard what was being communicated.

Electrical engineers have a great slogan: *reduce the noise and capture the signal*. That's a pretty succinct statement of the heart of mindful communication. Sometimes the noise is the many distractions that prevent our minds from fully attending. We miss some of what is being said because our attention drifts or is pulled away, even when we are sitting across the desk from someone and looking straight at him. We don't listen to that other person, and we often don't listen to ourselves. As we saw with Beth and Catherine, if Beth hadn't paused long enough to take in what she was feeling, her reactive mind would have taken over that meeting—with a very different outcome.

Sometimes the noise is in our own heads. How many times have you noticed that much of what is said in a meeting is redundant? We ask ourselves how he could ask that question when it was answered five minutes ago or make the same comment someone made ten minutes ago. Or we wonder if she's even in the room when she says something completely unrelated to the current topic. What is going on? Are the participants in these meetings simply not listening?

When we are so engrossed in planning our next comment or wording our next question, it's difficult to remain attentive to what's being said. When we add to all that mental preparation work the need to find an opening to speak in a fast-paced meeting, it becomes virtually impossible really to hear and then take in what someone is saying. All that noise keeps us from listening. The productivity loss from such wasted communications can be draining and costly. On the other hand, when we are able to stay focused on listening and redirect our attention when the mind becomes entangled in the noise, then we're able to take in the complete signal. Imagine the efficiency if we had everyone's attention in meetings. Imagine the improved quality of those meetings if we took the time to listen and then speak truthfully about the topics at hand. I have yet to meet an employee or leader who does not believe that a typical day contains too many meetings and that most of them waste huge amounts of time. Can mindful communication training help?

Gregory Kramer, author of *Insight Dialogue*, offers a mindful communication methodology that has been adapted for use in mindful leadership training. It involves a four-step process, which can occur in a matter of seconds once the practice has become ingrained.

The first step is to *pause*. In the pause, you have an opportunity to check in with yourself. You can use the sensations of your breath or the feeling of your feet on the floor to ground you to the present so that you enter the communication with your whole being—mind, body, and heart.

The second step is to *open to what is here, actually here, rather than what you imagined or hoped would be here.* This may sound like an easy step, but it can be the most difficult. You take your life experiences into each encounter you enter, so you often bring expectations into a conversation that can interfere with hearing what someone is saying. As a leader, you may carry so much responsibility for meeting goals and making numbers that this pressure can filter your ability to hear messages that are unexpected. In today's world, changes happen rapidly, and at any given moment we may find ourselves facing conditions that are different from the ones we knew before. Markets may change (think of late 2008); physical conditions may change (think of a flu outbreak or a tsunami); personal circumstances may change (think of Catherine's crisis). It's imperative that each of us cultivate the ability to be open to what is here so we can be flexible and efficient—and so we can be compassionate and skillful in our choices, as we saw in Beth's story.

The third step is to *listen deeply* and redirect your attention when you notice the quality of your attention waning. This includes listening to yourself, to the sensations and thoughts arising as you listen to others speaking. You need full attention to take in what others are communicating: the words, the body language, the felt emotions—the full richness of a connection.

The fourth step is to *speak the truth with the intention to do no harm*. As leaders, we need to value and encourage this fourth step, and it requires more than an invitation for colleagues and teams to do so. It requires a culture that truly makes it safe for each person to speak his or her truth.

I have only seen this done effectively when a leader models the behavior. For example, if a leader treats "bad news" as an opportunity for everyone to learn and for the organization to become more resilient rather than as a career-damaging event, the truth will quickly become an important part of the dialogue.

As the culture becomes more familiar with customarily speaking the truth, it is increasingly important that speakers understand they have an obligation to be sure they always speak with the intention to do no harm. Speaking the truth is not a license to be insulting or denigrating, nor should it be done solely to advance one's career. The purpose of speaking the truth in mindful communication is to be beneficial or of service to colleagues, the organization, or the community.

However, when leaders make a genuine commitment to fostering honesty, speaking the truth can also advance one's career, as we will see in an example from Ford Motor Company. Alan Mulally was named the CEO of Ford in 2006, a time when the company was losing billions of dollars per year. Each week, he gathered his team members for an update meeting. Mulally asked each executive to use a traffic light system to assess progress:

green if all was well, *yellow* to signal some concerns, and *red* to indicate a significant problem. For the first few months of his tenure, when Mulally asked for their updates, the managers each held up green lights, even as the company kept slipping. Mulally was more than a little frustrated. Finally, one manager, Mark Fields, raised the first red signal. We can imagine heads swiveling and eyes widening at the conference table when Fields admitted trouble. The CEO's response: "Great visibility, Mark. Is there anything we can do to help you?" Fields would go on to turn around Ford's North American business from record losses to record profit in four years, and in fall 2012, he was named COO. Mulally had invited truth, and when Fields took a chance to see if that invitation was authentic, Alan Mulally walked the talk.

On the other hand, when truth is not an expected part of everyday dialogue, it is sometimes because employees have the belief that no one wants to hear bad news, and that only people who are not team players offer a different point of view. While they may seem smooth on the surface, these organizational cultures feel stifled, the employees are less engaged, and the organization is less innovative. Truth often offers us resistance, and resistance is good. As Maya Lin, the architect for the Vietnam Memorial, once said, "Without resistance, we cannot fly."

MINDFUL COMMUNICATION—LISTENING TO YOURSELF

The way to learn mindful communication is by applying it to the everyday situations you encounter in your work and your life. A good place to begin is by trying some exercises that prepare you for what you will face in the heat of the moment. This first exercise invites you to become more familiar with how your mind and body respond to words, and what insights you might gather from those responses.

Sit comfortably and slowly read the following list of mindful behaviors and their definitions. Be particularly attentive to sensations in the body. Do you notice any tightening? Do certain terms resonate with you? Notice as well the thoughts and emotions that the list may trigger. Bring a curiosity to whatever you are noticing, without any need to analyze it or push it away.

Acceptance: seeing, feeling, and acknowledging things as
they are in the present moment. Acceptance does not mean
passivity, resignation, or agreement. It allows a clear
perception of the present that informs our actions.

Letting go: allowing change to occur by not holding on to
thoughts, feelings, and experiences. It is an intentional act
and does not mean suppression or forgetfulness.

Openness: perceiving things as if for the first time; remaining
aware of attitudes and opinions that may block such fresh
perception.

Generosity: giving in the present moment within a context of
care and compassion, without need for gain, recognition,
or return.

Suspending judgment: impartial witnessing; observing
the present moment by moment without evaluation and
categorization.

Empathy: the quality of feeling and understanding another
person's situation in the present moment, inclusive of their
perspectives, emotions, and actions.

Nonstriving: remaining unattached to outcome or
achievement; not forcing things by holding on or pushing
away.

Gentleness: consideration and tenderness. Gentleness,
however, is not passive, unassertive, or indulgent.

In reading the list, did you find that certain words evoked bodily sensations? A warmth in the heart? A tightening in the chest? What thoughts popped into your head along with those sensations? Did judgments arise? By exploring them, you're beginning to appreciate the workings of your mind as you are taking in information. In essence, you are practicing listening to yourself.

MINDFUL COMMUNICATION—LISTENING TO OTHERS

You can extend this practice by pairing up with a partner and practicing listening to each other.

In this exercise, each person reads through the list of qualities above and then shares the experience of listening to his or her own body and mind while reading the page. Instead of having a discussion, partners take turns. Each partner has up to five minutes (using all or any part of that time) to give a monologue about the experience. The listening partner's job is to do just that: to listen, without interrupting with questions or comments, and also to be aware of his or her own responses. Then the roles are reversed and the process repeated.

This simple exercise often reveals intriguing insights about the ways we communicate. Participants notice the relief they feel from just listening without having to work on a polite response or add a significant comment. They also notice that, although it could feel awkward at first not to interject little assurances to show that they were listening, the lack of those head nods and "uh-huh" comments did nothing to diminish the connection between the partners.

As for the experience of speaking in monologue, people often notice that speaking without the need to get it out quickly before someone interrupts allows them to go deeper and deeper into what they are saying and discover more about the significance of what they are noticing. Finally, in the spaciousness of a few-minute monologue, participants report being more likely to speak the truth because their thoughts and emotions were more clearly heard and understood, by themselves and by their listening partners.

It's not so easy for us to communicate mindfully, especially about matters that have emotional content. It takes some effort and application. We have decades of conditioning to overcome. Yet a little bit of practice with exercises like the one above can help us begin to notice how much of the time we are simply *hearing*, not *listening*. We lose something important when we're not fully present for an encounter with people we're close to, whether spouse, child, or colleague: we lose the precious opportunity to understand and to be understood.

PREPARED TO REALLY LISTEN

Dave was an innovation expert at a major consumer products company and had been entrusted with bringing a new product line to market. The project was on a fast track, with a goal of introducing it by the third quarter, about four months away. Things were progressing well, and he and the fifteen-member team he was leading were on track to meet their deadline. In fact, they were probably going to beat it by a few weeks.

Dave began his Monday morning team meeting with the usual spin around the room, allowing the leaders to speak about progress and whatever issues they were facing. Halfway through, though, as he listened more deeply to what he was hearing, Dave began to pick up on an uneasy feeling. Since they were so clearly going to meet their objectives, he wondered why he didn't sense more enthusiasm and excitement from the group. The updates sounded perfunctory and flat. He stopped midstream. Rather than just "getting it done" or even checking the accuracy of what he was feeling with the team, he decided to trust his instincts. Dave asked the group just one question: "If it were solely up to you, would you bring this product to market?" He invited the group to take a couple of moments to really consider the question. When he thought the group was ready, he gave each person three minutes to present an honest assessment, his or her truth, in an uninterrupted monologue.

By the time they were halfway around the table, the team members knew the right thing to do was to halt the project. Although they could bring the line to market, there were many reasons not to do so, ranging from increased costs (which meant a lesser-quality product to stay within budget) to a sense that the product was no longer at the standard of excellence in innovation that the group felt capable of creating if given more time.

This kind of courageous act in a corporate setting requires leadership presence. Dave's courage was supported by his training in mindful communication. Once more, here are the four steps in the process:

1. Pause
2. Open to what is here
3. Listen deeply
4. Speak the truth

Dave took these principles into a routine meeting, challenging the group to stop and speak honestly about the product. Mindful communication and mindful leadership require that we trust the feelings that invite us to inquire more deeply about the situations we find ourselves in, rather than just completing tasks and checking off boxes. Dave's understanding and practice of mindful leadership helped him to model a way of leading that was not afraid to listen to what was really going on, rather than just gloss over it in the interest of meeting a deadline—and to change course on the spot. He also sent the message that he was really interested in listening to what people were saying. He chose to stop the routine to see and feel what was in the room. He allowed each member of the team to deliver a short monologue, then posed a question that would leave open the option of choosing to abandon the path they had been on for many months. All of these choices created a safe opportunity for each person to be heard. Above all, Dave led by developing an atmosphere that valued honesty and excellence.

The remainder of that Monday morning meeting was spent working on a better idea for a new product. It would take a few days, and a few more meetings, but the team soon found a product that they could deliver, and that they believed would be a better performer. Dave still had to explain the change in direction to his manager, and the fact that the product launch would need to be postponed from the third quarter until the fourth. While the delay was unwelcome news, it was offset by the innovation of the new product and the projections for its success.

Is Dave's story familiar? How many times have you been in a meeting when everyone knows that the project is no longer a good idea? Or should no longer be a priority because a change in the market has occurred? Or should be modified because it is not the best choice for the environment? Perhaps people make some comments in the hallways or behind closed doors but not in the conference room. Perhaps team members have the same questions as the leader of the project but have convinced themselves that they are too far down the road to make a change. I call these moments times when we are busy talking to ourselves. We're going to great lengths to convince ourselves that what we are doing is still right. These are the moments when being fully present and listening to all that is said and unsaid in the room can be a valuable act of leadership.

THE NOISE OF MULTITASKING

What effect does multitasking have on mindful communication? A quick look at a common type of experience with this may provide some important insights. You have an important meeting to update your boss on a key project at 10 A.M., and when you arrive, he tells you to go ahead although he may need to ask you to step out for a few minutes if an overseas call he is expecting comes through. You begin to give him your update but notice that every so often he glances at the clock and checks his e-mail. In between the glances, however, he makes eye contact with you and nods his head periodically so it seems as though he is hearing what you are saying. Nevertheless, you finish the meeting knowing full well that he listened to virtually nothing.

When you're speaking with someone who's not really paying attention, you can feel the distractedness, and you don't feel the connection that is so apparent when someone is really listening to what you have to say. When someone is multitasking, participating in a meeting with one eye on a clock or laptop or smartphone, for example, it is not only less productive because the communication will likely need repeating at some point, it is disrespectful. I knew of one corporate president who would begin his division meetings by telling everyone to turn off all laptops and phones. He would then say, "If you have something more pressing to do with this hour than participate in this division meeting, go take care of it and return when you can be a full participant." Now that sets a tone.

When I began to practice mindful communication more deliberately, I was astonished by how many times in a day I would catch my mind wandering off during a meeting or during a chat with a colleague or friend. And I began to notice how difficult it was to connect with someone and really hear what that person was saying when I had one eye on my computer or some other distraction. Perhaps one of the most vivid realizations of this came when I was having a conversation with my daughter, then a teenager. She and I would routinely prepare dinner together, and I would ask her about her day. One evening as we were working at the counter cutting up some carrots and celery, she was telling me about a fight her friend was having with another girl. Midway through the story, I began to hear some hesitancy in her voice, and it occurred to me that I was multitasking, trying to listen to the details of her story as I was preparing dinner. I put down my knife and turned to face her. Her response was to take a little jump back, startled by this increase in attention. Then her whole body seemed to soften, and she, too, put down her work to turn toward me and continue the story with ease and openness. It was an important lesson for me. The depth of connection I have with others, at home and at work, is directly affected by my capacity to pay attention, and then to speak, or listen, from the mind and heart.

Most of the people I've met who seek mindful leadership training believe they communicate well. After all, they're highly accomplished in their fields. Most have been through training to strengthen their ability to be clear and precise when speaking about a topic, or to motivate and excite an audience with inspirational language. These are common abilities for those identified by an organization as a leader, or as someone who has high potential. However, this kind of training often leaves out the other side of the equation, the side that trains the mind and body to *listen closely to what is being said*. Whether in a negotiation, a performance review, a strategy session, or the informal dialogue that is at the heart of any organization, noticing when you are simply not in the room can mean the difference between excellence and just putting the tick marks next to the items on your to-do list. The more responsibility you have, the more people you are leading and the larger the scope of your leadership, the more important it becomes to clear away the noise so you can listen to your wisdom and speak from the mind and heart—and, as importantly, so you can listen to what others are saying, and what they are not saying.

PURPOSEFUL PAUSE: MINDFUL MEETING

As you walk to your next meeting, bring attention to the sensations of your breath, redirecting your attention whenever you notice that it has wandered off. When you settle into your chair in the meeting room, become aware of the movements of your body as it bends at the waist, touches the chair, places the feet flat on the floor, picks up and holds a pen, and so on.

Form a strong intention to pay full attention to what is being said. Remain open and curious about what will be unfolding rather than fixing on an expectation about what will happen. During the meeting, whenever you notice that your mind has drifted, bring it back to the present by attending to the breath or the sensations in your body for a few moments, letting go of the discursive thoughts or judgments that interfere with really listening. Remember the four steps of mindful communication: pause, open to what is here, listen deeply, and, when it is your turn, speak truthfully (always with the intention to do no harm).

Afterward, take a moment to reflect on how you experienced the meeting. What did you notice—about you, about the others in the room, about the efficiency or inefficiency of the meeting? Is this a purposeful pause that you will make part of each meeting? Are there changes to the meeting process you might like to suggest? Was the meeting hijacked by a strong personality? Would a two-minute monologue have been helpful? Would a no-smartphone/no-laptop rule be a time-saver? Finally, did the culture of the meeting value honesty?

CHAPTER 7

Just Walk . . . Senses and Sensations

Small is the number of them that see with their own eyes and feel with their own hearts.

ALBERT EINSTEIN

SOMETIME TODAY YOU WERE PROBABLY walking from one place to another—to and from your car, to work, or simply down the hallway in the office. How much did you notice during your walk? Can you remember any details, or did it go by in a blur of your own thinking? Most of the time, we ignore the act of walking while we multitask, or we treat it as an impediment as we hurry from one appointment to the next. We would prefer to be beamed over to our next event, thus reclaiming the time we waste traveling by means of our own feet. We have become a society of moving heads—engrossed in our smartphones, or in our thoughts of the future and the past, paying little attention to the actual experience of walking.

Perhaps it is, in part, because we don't realize what we're missing. When we practice mindful walking, we begin to reconnect with our bodies and listen to the many messages they send. As we learned in Chapter 4, the sensory language of the body is a rich stream of information—not just the five senses we learned about as children, but also the gut feelings we became more familiar with as we grew and the sense that orients us to our surroundings, known as proprioception. Our senses interpret the world, both the external world of our physical environment, and the internal world of our thoughts and emotions.

An example of how walking meditation can put you in touch with the state of your body and be a fertile ground for insights to arise occurred during a program I was leading for a pharmaceutical company's top employees. We had just finished practicing some walking meditation outside and were returning to our chairs to speak about our experiences. Bashir, a middle-aged financial analyst, shared with us that during his practice he was surprised to notice that he was "exhausted"—not just tired from a busy life, but exhausted "down to the cellular level." Before the retreat, he didn't think he was even tired. Bashir sat quietly for a couple of minutes before adding, "This feeling is deep in my body, and it's not about missing sleep." As he got closer to what he had been noticing, he further described the feeling as a "weightiness" in his chest and a "tightness" in his throat. His surprise at these discoveries turned into an open curiosity about the source of these feelings that were draining his energy.

Bashir spent the next few days exploring these sensations and listening to the insights and emotions that began to arise. Slowly, he began to realize they were connected to his participation in the office politics of his company. The political landscape had intensified recently with the hiring of a new officer. Bashir began to question his choices to take on more and more responsibilities solely out of what he began to see was his fear that he would not continue to have his leadership position if he did not say yes to everything. He understood how the work he had loved had now become the weight that made it hard to get out of bed in the morning. If he hadn't stopped and allowed his body's messages to be heard, and then brought an open curiosity to what they meant, Bashir might have just pushed through. He might have ignored or misunderstood the very information that could help him look at how he was encountering his life and, most importantly, might help him make some skillful changes. The experience was a vivid lesson for all of us about the value of connecting with the sensations in the body.

MINDFUL WALKING MEDITATION

Although you can do mindful walking practice anywhere and at any time, it is usually helpful to begin exploring walking practice by choosing a relatively quiet place where you will be uninterrupted for ten or fifteen minutes. It can be indoors or outdoors. The place should have enough space for you to take several steps in a straight line. Beginning at one end of the straight path you have chosen, slowly begin to walk. There is no need to walk in a stylized way or excessively slowly, but I suggest walking a bit slower than your normal speed. When you reach the end of your path, pause for a moment or two, and then turn and walk back. There is no need to look at your feet. Gaze straight ahead, taking in the landscape right in front of you. Your arms can comfortably hang by your side, or be clasped in front of you or behind you. As you turn, take in the panorama as you continue to look straight ahead. That's it for the mechanics.

As for your mind, notice the sensations we have been talking about in this chapter. The information your body is gathering through its many senses is all here for you to notice: sights, sounds, the weight shifting from one foot to the other. You may also notice the internal workings of your body—pains and strains, hunger, tiredness.

You just walk and know that you are walking. You may notice the feelings in your calf muscle as your foot flexes, the pressure on your heel as it strikes the ground, the touch of the air on your skin, the colors of the landscape ahead of you, or the tightness in your chest. When your thinking mind is pulled away from the experience of just walking, redirect your attention to focus on where you are and what you are doing.

Walking in this very mindful way isn't about getting anywhere; it's about training the mind to be present for the journey. Just as you did with meditations with the breath and sounds, and with the desk chair meditation, when you notice the mind has wandered, bring it back to the sensations, firmly and gently, with discipline and with compassion. The redirecting of your attention is the practice and helps to stabilize and concentrate your mind.

This can be a challenging practice at first since most of us are unaccustomed to walking without distracting ourselves with conversation, a cell phone or MP3 player, or our own thinking. When you intentionally limit those distractions, you are in your own good company for a while, and you see up close just how your mind and body experience something as simple as walking, without any other project to occupy yourself. You may notice frustration because you often walk very quickly, while in this practice you walk more slowly than usual. This frustration itself can be fruitful. It can give you an opportunity to deepen your intention to practice. Rather than giving up because you don't want to feel the emotions, you can use them as part of the training. When frustration arises, you can recognize that feeling, and then pay attention to the sensations that are arising with it. In this way, you are investigating the qualities of frustration itself, noticing whatever arises as you continue to practice.

Or perhaps you notice a strain in your neck accompanied by a flood of judgmental thoughts. Rather than react to the content of those thoughts, continue to train the mind by attending to the sensations, just as they are in that moment. This gives you a chance to observe how you react to difficulty and change. By giving yourself some space in this way, you can experiment with choosing to meet those sensations differently. You might, for example, choose to simply notice them, intentionally let go of the judgmental thoughts that arise, and continue to practice.

For some people, mindful walking opens a flood of discoveries, or perhaps more accurately rediscoveries. When you're doing the basic practice of walking back and forth in a line, the freedom of simply walking without a destination opens the door to noticing once again the wonderful sounds, smells, and sights that often surround you: the chirping of a bird, the rustling of the leaves, the smell of newly mown grass. The simple pleasures and joys you might have experienced as a child are still available to be rediscovered, and you can take great delight in that.

As you become more familiar with walking meditation, you can use this practice during any walk, at any speed. For example, if you notice your mind racing as you hurriedly walk to your next meeting, bring your attention to the feeling of your heel striking the hallway floor as you walk. Every time your mind takes off to thoughts about the meeting, redirect your attention back to the body's sensations. Arriving fully in the present may make it more likely that you will be a valuable participant in the meeting. Or, if you have the chance to go for a Sunday afternoon walk and notice that you are still thinking about your Friday morning meeting, use the mindful walking training to redirect your attention to the body's sensations. Walk and be aware that you are on a walk.

Walking meditation can be added to your daily meditation practice, either as an additional ten-minute practice each day or as an alternative to a sitting practice. Be patient with yourself. This is another new way to train the mind, and it may take a while to become accustomed to the training.

A WALK IN THE WOODS

In the mindful walking practice, we're cultivating the capacity to bring awareness to everything we experience as we simply pay attention to the movement of the body through its surroundings. We can also listen to the sensations of the heart—joy's lightness in the chest, fear's tightening, grief's weightiness, love's physical warmth, and so on. We begin to remember the richness of being awake, fully embodied in this moment. Most importantly, as we will see in the following example, when we fail to pay attention to these sensations, we can miss out on the joy and insights that can arise when we more fully experience life and are more receptive to the messages coming from all of our senses.

I was with a group of leaders on retreat in Minnesota. After an early-morning meditation practice, we ate breakfast and were set to begin a full day of silent practice—mindful movement, sitting practice, and walking practice. The previous two days had been rainy, and we all had a bit of cabin fever. I was hopeful that we would spend much of this day outside. The early morning was still a bit foggy, but it wasn't raining, so we began the morning with a mindful walk on the nearby trails.

As we passed a tall pine tree, I mentioned that the enormous nest near the top belonged to a pair of bald eagles, although the eagles did not appear to be home. We paused to take in the beauty of its architecture and then started walking past the tree. A few yards down the path, the retreat assistant whispered in my ear that the eagle was perched on the back side of the tree, on a branch behind the nest we had just viewed from the other side. As I turned, there she was, in full view, motionless, just gazing over the landscape—a stunningly beautiful, majestic bald eagle. We stopped and turned around to take in this amazing sight.

We stood together, shoulder to shoulder, silently sharing this moment only a few feet from the tree. We felt connected—to each other, to the presence of this magnificent symbol of freedom, to

the beauty of nature all around us. And we felt connected to ourselves, our senses keenly taking it all in. We were silent and still
and in awe. It was not lost on any of us that this incredible moment might so easily have been missed if we were rushing by in
our usual way.

After a while, the eagle began to ruffle its feathers, arch its
back, and lift its wings. I could feel a sense of anticipation rising
in the group as we wondered if we would get to see the huge bird
take flight, rising high into the sky. Instead, she lifted her tail
feathers and proceeded to relieve herself, sending a bucket's worth
of urine cascading through the branches. The silence of the group
was interrupted by a collective gasp that quickly dissolved into
spontaneous laughter. In that moment, we experienced together a
childlike moment of utter surprise and delight.

The eagle, however, was not done putting on a show. As the
laughter subsided and the eagle resumed her watchful silence, I
began to wonder if it was time for us to continue on with our
walking, but somehow I still felt it was better to be patient. A few
minutes later, we heard and then saw the eagle's mate heading
toward the branch, screeching his arrival. They greeted each other
with cries for a few moments, and then, as we were fully transfixed on the rare encounter we were witnessing, the eagles proceeded to mate. This was enough to send our group into laughter
that brought tears to our eyes. There was no need for words.

A few minutes later, as this second round of laughter died
down and we still stood completely motionless, transfixed on the
eagles, the female spread her wings and took flight, effortlessly
sailing in a large circle around the group and then disappearing
into the morning's misty sky. We stood for a while longer, and
then slowly we began to walk away from the pine tree, leaving the
male eagle to resume his silent gaze on the landscape.

When we ended the period of silence later that day and began
talking, many people spoke of their experience that morning.
Marcia, one of the most senior executives on the retreat, spoke

about her unexpected discovery. "As I watched the eagles," she said, "I was reminded of how we hold the eagle in such high esteem. We put it on a pedestal because it stands for all the aspirational virtues of our country. I felt the strength and stillness of the eagles as we watched them. And I also saw that eagles are messy, and that messy is okay." Her words resonated with many of us. Leaders often believe that we need to embody certain ideals and always be "buttoned up," not allowing ourselves to appear unknowing or unsure. But life is messy, and messy is okay. In fact, welcoming the messy parts is an important part of leading, of innovating, of accepting our vulnerability, of living our lives. Just ask an eagle.

CHAPTER 8

Discovering Your Leadership Principles

You have to leave the city of your comfort and go into the wilderness of your intuition . . . What you'll discover will be wonderful. What you'll discover is yourself.

ALAN ALDA

IT'S A COLD JANUARY MORNING, and the week begins with a 9 A.M. meeting in the company's auditorium. The executives are all sitting in the front row, and the CEO is walking toward the stage. He begins his talk by reminding everyone that the company had a good year but the market is changing and it is now time to look ahead to new objectives. And, he tells the employees, the Organizational Effectiveness Department has developed a set of new leadership principles designed to help everyone with the execution of the new strategies to meet those objectives.

Sound familiar?

A large-screen version of the leadership principles is unveiled, typically a list of words and phrases, perhaps tucked into a circle design or a pyramid, and carefully color-coded. The list might include words like *ethics*, *innovation*, *inclusiveness*, and *service*. Or it might be a list of leadership principles like these:

1. We will maintain high ethical standards in delivering our services to the client.
2. We will execute our business plan flawlessly, valuing our capacity to be flexible and innovative.
3. We will foster an environment of inclusion and mutual respect.

Someone from the C-suite reinforces the importance of the list.

Each person walks out of the meeting with a pocket version of the new leadership principles and maybe even a screensaver application for his computer or an app for her phone. The list is meant to be inspiring and unifying, and it is meant to clearly communicate the expectations the company leadership has for itself and for its employees. While it is important for employees to understand that there are such expectations and that certain principles of doing business are valued by the organization, is a communication like this enough to ensure that those principles guide the day-to-day decisions?

Have you ever been asked about your leadership principles?

What are they?

Why is it important that you know?

In this chapter, we will use mindful leadership training to help us answer these questions, beginning with a reflection.

REFLECTION ON LEADERSHIP PRINCIPLES

> ▶ To begin this reflection, you will need to take a paper and pen with you to a quiet, private space. Take a seated meditation posture with your feet on the floor, back straight, hands comfortably in your lap or on your thighs, and eyes closed or with a soft downward gaze.

Bring your attention to your breath, feeling the sensations of the in-breath and the out-breath. Allow the practice with the breath to cultivate a concentration and steadiness in your mind, redirecting your attention as often as it wanders.

As your body and mind settle into the stillness, silently ask yourself about your principles:

What are my leadership principles?
What principles are at the core of who I am and how I want to lead?
What principles am I passionate about?
What principles form the rudder that I can turn to when the complexities of life serve up a rocky sea?

Be open and curious. Leave space for the answers to arise. You can choose to ask yourself these questions one at a time, noticing what responses come up, or you can group them together and then notice what arises.

Set aside the first few reflexive responses, and let go of the discursive mind that may begin to analyze the questions. Rather, allow time and space for responses to arise from deep within. The answers already exist; they just might take a little time to work their way through the busy mind and the years of being told how to be a successful leader. Pay attention to any bodily sensations you may notice during the reflection. They may be helpful in discovering your answers to the questions. Be patient.

When you are ready, open your eyes and write down your responses. Don't bother assessing what arose. Stay attentive to any bodily sensations. Perhaps you will notice uneasiness in the body, a lightness in the chest, or a tightness in the neck as you write your responses. Be curious about what those sensations might mean. Are the sensations familiar? When else do you notice them? Are you surprised by what arose as your leadership principles?

In mindful leadership workshops and retreats, I have heard leaders sharing their experience with this reflection relate to the group that they were caught off guard by some of the words that came up from within themselves. They were not the typical execution-oriented characteristics that they recognize as part of their work each day. The reflection instead, gave voice to another, deeper trait of leading with excellence. Here is a sample of their leadership principles:

Kindness
A thirst for true discovery
Truth
Fairness
Desire to pass along experiences
Generosity
Making the world a better place
Respect for everyone
Love
Excellence
Willingness to experiment, and learn from failures

The leadership principles identified by an organization are guidelines for how the senior leadership in that company wants the organization to do business. The assumption is that if everyone behaves in accordance with these principles, there is a better chance that the company will be successful. That is an important goal. There is a big difference, however, between being told how to behave and discovering leadership principles for yourself.

When you discover them, they are authentically yours. You recognize that they are central to some important ways that you wish to live your life, and you bring them into the workplace. When you discover them for yourself, they are a part of you from the inside out. Their influence on your decisions and behaviors in the midst of the daily chaos is likely to be much greater than an organization telling you to behave a certain way. This may seem obvious, but why is it that the opportunity to discover your personal leadership principles is so rarely included in the development of leaders?

A vital element within mindful leadership practice is coming to a deeper understanding of yourself, and understanding your leadership principles is a key part of that self-knowledge. Knowing those principles—and becoming more curious about them and how they define who you are—is the compass that will guide you when faced with difficult choices. It is a way for you to reassess your priorities and to see whether, in the choices you're making, you are embodying your principles of leadership or standing in the way of their full expression.

Most of us have never been asked about our leadership principles or taken the time to know what they are. You may want to spend a few of your daily meditation practices with this reflection. Keep adding to your list, and remain open and curious about what arises. It might also be useful to talk about them and their importance to you with a trusted friend. Giving voice to your principles is another way for you to learn about them. This is time well spent. If you work long enough, you will undoubtedly find yourself in situations where tough choices need to be made. In the pressure and heat of that moment, you do not want to be searching to discover your principles.

WHY IS IT IMPORTANT FOR YOU TO IDENTIFY YOUR LEADERSHIP PRINCIPLES?

There is really no such thing as an organization.

The organization exists only as a piece of paper in a state office. An organization is a shifting, dynamic, interactive collection of people. The organization *is run by* employees or volunteers, *serves* consumers or clients or patients, *is invested in* by shareholders or contributors, and *answers to* shareholders or boards. These people make the decisions that create the role the organization plays in the community, for better or worse. If we want organizations to behave with a greater level of awareness, we need to invite the people who are the organization to begin to explore more about themselves and their innate capacities. This exploration begins with an invitation to get closer to, to discover or uncover, the principles they hold. When this understanding is missing or forgotten, the likelihood that each of us will act in mindless or negligent ways is much greater.

A vivid example of this was shared with me a couple of years ago. Olivia, an officer in the sales division of a large publicly-traded electronics company, was once again leading her team into the closing of the quarter. While everyone else went home for a long holiday weekend, her team would be tallying up the numbers on Saturday and getting the final orders through before the 8 P.M. deadline. Public companies have to adhere to strict accounting guidelines to avoid even the appearance that quarterly numbers are being fiddled with to manipulate the valuation of the stock by analysts and the public.

The team had worked a twelve-hour day, and they were almost done. One of Olivia's middle managers, Becky, was new to the division and was eager to show her worth to her new colleagues. Minutes after the accounting books were closed to new orders, and sent to Olivia and the accounting offices, Becky took a call for a large new order. If this order could be booked in the current quarter, it would be the difference between making the projected numbers for the quarter and missing them. Becky thought she could simply go back into the computer and quickly modify the sales figures for the quarter. It was just a little past the close. Why not? It had been a tough year for the company, and management put enormous pressure on the sales division to meet the quarter's projections. Everyone would be happy that Becky had obtained this new order and found a way at the last minute to not disappoint the investment analysts.

Becky went to find Olivia to ask her about the idea of slipping the order into the quarter that had been closed. She found her with one hand on the phone to accounting and one hand rifling through some orders on her desk. Olivia looked up for a minute and waved Becky into her office. She finished her call and then half-listened as Becky explained what she proposed to do.

The phone rang again just as Becky finished telling Olivia what she had in mind. The president of the division was asking for a status report, and Olivia was anxious to take the call, so she simply said, "If you have any ideas to make the sales numbers better for the quarter, go ahead." Becky went to the computer and altered the order sheet in violation of public accounting standards.

Fortunately, for the company's sake, the accounting office detected the violation before a false quarterly report was released, but the story did not end there. The company launched an internal investigation into how this could have happened, and it resulted in a recommendation that Olivia be dismissed, and that the entire team undergo retraining in proper reporting procedures. Olivia later tearfully admitted that she "knew better." She said, "Honesty and integrity are so important to me. I've been doing this for more than ten years and I would never think of violating the rules we have in place. But the pressure to meet our projections was so strong and so much was at stake that in the heat of the moment I forgot who I was."

The more we understand about our principles, the closer we become to them. And the closer we become to them, the less likely it will be that, in the heat of the moment, we will forget who we are. When good people make ethical or legal mistakes, or violate a company's internal procedures, it isn't because they aren't smart or well trained, it is because they didn't listen to their own wisdom. The discovery and understanding of our principles gets us

closer to hearing that wisdom. Mistakes like Olivia's, and countless others we often read about in the media, occur in a matter of
minutes, but such acts can ruin careers, hurt families, and set off a
chain reaction of negative effects that touch countless other people.

Of course, there are people who intentionally make unethical
decisions and who may not have that inner wisdom (or have
pushed it out of their consciousness). In my experience, though,
the truly devious people are the exceptions and perhaps are so
self-absorbed that they are incapable of knowing the devastation
their choices will cause. For most of us, reconnecting with our
principles will lessen the chances that we will fail to hear the voice
that will help us make the right choice in difficult situations.

When you have had the space to identify and examine your
leadership principles, it is more likely that you will be able to access
them in those moments when the choice is unclear, or when there
is an opportunity to change the routine. Your principles help you
to find the strength to make the tough choices, to take the risks
often inherent in innovation or to open your heart to the suffering
of others.

We have already seen some examples of leadership principles
in action. In Chapter 1, leadership principles influenced the choice
to recall the chocolate candy, and in Chapter 6, Beth's strongly
held compassion principle guided her choice to ask Catherine,
"Are you okay?" In both stories, the leaders were under pressure
and could have made a different choice. If the recall team or Beth
were less connected to their principles—if, for example, they were
only interested in the short-term execution of objectives or quarterly returns—those situations might have had a very different result. Bringing your leadership principles into your decision-making
process does not negate everything else you need to consider, but
it does help you to see a fuller picture of the options available to
you. It helps you make the best decisions possible.

CHAPTER 9

Seeing Thoughts and Emotions Clearly

I've been through some terrible things in my life, some of which actually happened.

ATTRIBUTED TO MARK TWAIN

IN HIS TYPICALLY UNDERSTATED fashion, Twain suggests in this quip just how much our own thoughts create worry, anxiety, and stress that are terribly real, even if the threat that gave rise to them is wholly or largely imaginary. We can write entire novels in our minds about what is going to happen or what might happen sometime in the future. We become clairvoyant and "know" what others are thinking or saying or planning. We launch into critical analyses of ourselves that include standards that are not humanly possible to meet. In the process, our thoughts carry us away from being present for what is in our life right now.

We give our thoughts too much weight. We often take them as gospel truth when, in fact, they are simply random ideas that may or may not be true. In the development of leadership excellence, the next step in training the mind invites us to use thoughts as the objects of attention. This meditation helps us to understand *the process of thinking*. It allows us to begin to notice our own thoughts a little less concretely and so creates some room for us to see them more clearly and to make a choice about what, if anything, should be our response.

MEDITATION WITH THOUGHTS AND EMOTIONS

In earlier chapters, the daily meditation practice focused on the variety of ways your body experiences and interprets the world. You have used the breath, sounds, and other bodily sensations as objects of attention. In this practice, you begin to use first thoughts and then emotions as objects of attention, training the mind using the same process outlined in Chapter 4. Begin by recalling the four steps for a daily meditation practice:

1. Find a comfortable seated position, allowing your body to become still and feel supported. You don't need meditation cushions, although you can certainly choose to use them. A straight-back chair works fine.
2. Identify an object for your attention. For the practices in this chapter you will be using thoughts or emotions as the objects of attention.
3. Bring an open curiosity to whatever you notice as you intentionally direct your attention to the object. Be open and curious about what arises. There is no need to change or control or assess what you are noticing.
4. Notice when your attention is pulled away or drifts away from the object you have chosen, and redirect your attention back to the object, without any judgments about how well you are doing with the practice.

AWARENESS OF THOUGHTS

▶ It is helpful to begin the practice by bringing attention to the breath for a few minutes. Then, as you are ready, let go of the breath sensations as the object of attention, and bring your attention to your thoughts as they arise and dissolve. This is not an invitation to *think*. It is an invitation to notice the *process of thinking*. Notice a thought as just that, a thought. We have a tendency to believe our thoughts are more than simply a "secretion of the mind," as Jon Kabat-Zinn has described them. In fact, our thoughts may or may not be compassionate, they may or may not be aligned with our values, they may or may not be accurately judging a situation or a person, and they certainly are not "us." We are much bigger than our thoughts. If that were not true, how could you notice when a thought arises during a meditation practice?

As you practice, you may notice a thought about the weather, an item on your to-do list, a memory from college. There is no need to *do* anything with the thought. Just notice it as it arises, and notice it as it dissolves and perhaps a different thought arises. Whether you notice an individual thought followed by empty space or an avalanche of thinking, one thought quickly followed by another, just practice with openness and curiosity about the process of thinking. This practice is not about emptying the mind, or changing what is happening. It is not a "better meditation" if you notice yourself having fewer thoughts. This practice is to notice what is here, whatever it is, and however it is.

The fact that certain thoughts tend to generate other thoughts may affect your practice. Rather than noticing the arising and dissolving of thoughts, you react to a given thought with more thinking. You may begin problem solving or planning next steps, or unpacking the substance of a thought. When you notice this is happening, simply let go of the train of thoughts and return to noticing the process of thinking.

In this practice, you are cultivating a different way of relating to what arises in your mind. Rather than analyzing every thought, or reacting to every thought, or thinking more thoughts about a thought, you are simply allowing your mind to rest in the awareness of thinking. In this practice, you are creating a space in which you might see your thoughts with greater clarity. Such clarity can help you make more intentional choices about which thoughts to respond to and which to simply let go. It can help you begin to see your conditioned reactivity and the thoughts that may be draining your energy or shrinking your potential for creativity or compassion.

Practicing with our thoughts in this way can make it easier to notice those times when there seems to be an inner battle between our intuition and our thinking mind. Marcel, a French entrepreneur and author, described this struggle.

> I had a very successful business that was just at the beginnings of its growth trajectory. I enjoyed the work, and yet there was a nagging feeling deep inside of me that it was time to sell it. To my most trusted colleagues, this idea was crazy. Why would I even think of doing that when all my hard work was now set to pay off? But I felt a strong pull at times to do something different with my life, although I didn't really know what that would look like. For several weeks, I just kept practicing with this uncertainty, noticing my thoughts—doubts, criticisms, judgments. And on occasion, I would feel more clearly the sense that it was time to move on. Finally the decision became clear. I would sell. And on the day I signed over the business, I noticed a surge of energy. The choice aligned with my core values and left me feeling very happy with the decision.

Ping-Pong Balls

This practice can also be especially important on those days when your mind seems about to explode with the number of thoughts bouncing around in your head. Phyllis, a vice president in a food science organization, described her experience with this practice in the midst of a very difficult day.

We were in the middle of an intensive audit of some potential safety concerns that had come to our management team's attention late in the day on Monday. We had too few resources in my department to handle the sudden flood of questions and demands for information. My calendar already had me triple-booked, and even though I arrived at 7 A.M. on Tuesday, ninety minutes earlier than usual, I had no idea how I was going to make it through all that had to be done. My calendar originally had me slated for the 8:30 A.M. mindfulness meditation practice we hold in our building every Tuesday, but I knew there was no way I could take thirty minutes for that practice today. So I jumped into the day with both feet and began to juggle the requests for information, the demands for speed, and the responsibility to make judgment calls about conflicting priorities.

But as it neared 8:30, I found myself rushing to the meditation conference room. I was a few minutes late and they had already started when I opened the door and collapsed into the chair. I began to practice with the sensations of my body and soon noticed the tightness in my neck and the shallowness of my breath. I noticed how often my attention was pulled away from my breath.

As we were guided to shift the practice to our thoughts, I noticed an image of thousands of Ping-Pong balls, each a thought, bouncing around in my head. As I began to practice, the balls seemed to settle into a stream and flow past me. As the practice continued, I was also aware that my breath had now settled into my belly and my neck was less tight. When the bells rang to mark the end of the practice, I was able to reach into that stream and make a conscious choice about the balls I needed to address first and the way I was going to approach the morning. I had found the space to lead with conscious choices instead of trying to react to every thought that was bouncing around in my head.

Phyllis's experience with meditation that morning helped her to notice the incessantly busy mind and allowed her to find a way to settle the busy-ness enough to make some conscious choices.

As you practice meditating with your thoughts as the object of your attention, you will also begin to become more aware of certain habitual behaviors and the thoughts that precede them. You will notice the opportunity to consciously choose what is next rather than react in the same way as you have in the past. Simon, a marketing president for a clothing chain, explained this experience to his mindful leadership colleagues at a recent practice session:

> I had been intentionally taking a purposeful pause at times throughout my day, especially noticing my typical thoughts and behaviors during my team's meetings. I used simple questions I had learned in the training to guide my experience:
>
> > What am I noticing about my mind and my body?
> > What's called for now?
>
> I began to find consistent answers to the first question. I noticed a kind of light tension in my body, as if I were on alert. And I noticed a steady stream of directions, ideas, and questions building up in my mind. But when I asked the second question, I almost always got the same answer: "Shut up!"

The leaders in the room smiled and nodded their heads. Simon continued:

> When I was in a meeting with my team, I would notice that thoughts of solutions to whatever problem we were discussing would arise, but if I took a moment to pause and ask myself

what the skillful choice right then was, I would notice the words "shut up" enter my head.

When I began to listen to that advice and resist the urge to jump in with my opinion, I saw that the team would discover new, and often better, ideas. And, importantly, I realized that I was genuinely advancing the development of each person on the team as they stretched and learned together. Letting go of jumping in too quickly to solve the problem based on what might have worked in the past created the space for the team to bring in new ideas. It served the business and it engaged the employees on the team.

AWARENESS OF EMOTIONS

We have seen that we can bring our attention to the process of thinking without any need to pile on more thoughts or assign to them more importance than they may be due. Similarly, we can practice with our emotions as objects of attention.

> Begin by practicing with the breath for a few minutes, and as you are ready, let the breath sensations fade into the background and bring your attention to emotions, noticing them as they arise and dissolve.
>
> Just like the breath, sound, and thoughts, emotions have a beginning and an end. This can be a challenging practice at first because few of us have been trained to be curious about our emotions. More likely, you have been taught to push them away, especially if they're uncomfortable. Sometimes, even knowing what you are feeling can be a challenge. So be patient with yourself.
>
> One helpful way to practice with emotions is to recognize that we often feel emotions in the body before we cognitively become aware of

them. For example, we notice a feeling of queasiness before we understand that we are nervous about this afternoon's year-end meeting with our manager. Or we notice the tears in our eyes before we identify them as the love we feel for our son as he walks across the stage at graduation. As we attend to emotions, we also begin to notice the bodily sensations associated with the emotions.

As you practice, you can relax into the meditation and just notice the emotions you're experiencing, just as they are. There is no need to bring thinking into the practice. For example, if you are practicing with emotions and you notice that you feel angry, simply notice that *this is anger.* There is no need to unpack the anger with discursive or analytical thinking like *why am I angry, I should really learn to forgive more, why is she so difficult, he did this on purpose,* and on and on and on. We are masters at this kind of thinking, and it is almost always unproductive. When this discourse begins, intentionally let it go and return to practicing with noticing emotions: *this is anger; this is where I notice anger in my body.*

You are not trying to push away the emotions. You are cultivating your ability to see and feel them more clearly so you can begin to understand yourself better or to choose a response to an emotion as it arises, rather than respond with a conditioned reaction. Emotions are an important part of who we are and how we meet the circumstances we encounter in our lives. In Chapter 12, we will explore further the role of emotions in leadership.

ADDING THE MEDITATION WITH THOUGHTS AND EMOTIONS TO YOUR DAILY PRACTICE

Bring these practices with thoughts and emotions into your daily meditation practice by including them with the others. For example, you might begin a session by practicing with your breath for a few minutes and then, when the mind feels stable and con-centrated, switch the object of attention to thoughts or emotions for the remainder of your practice. Or you might alternate prac-tices by, for example, practicing with the breath in the morning for ten minutes, and practicing with thoughts and emotions in the evening for ten minutes. You might also begin to expand your practice time by five or ten minutes each session as you begin to explore the meditation practices with thoughts and emotions. The extra time is often helpful in becoming more aware of your thinking process and in experiencing the wide range of emotions you are capable of feeling.

CHAPTER 10

Scheduling Space: The Urgent vs. the Important

What you do makes a difference, and you have to decide what kind of difference you want to make.

JANE GOODALL

"IT FEELS AS THOUGH I AM CONSTANTLY in the middle of an internal battle. There are aspects of my work and my life that I know are important, but they almost always seem to be pushed aside by the urgent. The trouble is, the urgent isn't usually as important, it just screams louder."

As Carey shared his frustration with a group of fellow employees, a chorus of heads nodded in agreement. When I asked him to tell us what he thought led to that situation, he paused for a while and said, "I guess the days just get away from me."

How do the days "just get away" from us? For most of us, it happens because we abdicate our responsibility to make clear choices about how we need to spend our time. We watch as we get booked, double-booked, and even triple-booked, then shrug our shoulders and accept it: "That's just the way it is." But does it need to be that way?

For example, rather than make a conscious choice, do you accept every meeting request on the assumption that if you are invited to a meeting, someone must think you are critically needed? Do you hold to that assumption even as you sit through frequent hour-long meetings only to realize that the meeting had little or nothing to do with what you needed to know about or accomplish?

Sometimes, our days get filled with "urgent" meetings because we have difficulty letting go and delegating responsibility to our team or to another department. We convince ourselves that our skills and experience will be needed and will result in what is most efficient and effective for all concerned. While there may be some truth to that, it is also true that today's world is very different from what it was even a few years ago, so fresh eyes unencumbered by the past may be an advantage. It is also true that developing people requires that we let go and let them learn and explore. Can we cultivate the discipline of taking a moment to decide when we need to go in person and when we can let others handle it, or be a coach or sounding board for others?

Sometimes, someone else's definition of "urgent" disrupts your calendar. Many years ago, when I was working for Nabisco, I was in a meeting with Miguel, a senior scientist, on a strategic project we were leading. About halfway through, Jon, a young employee, interrupted our conversation with an urgent need for an approval signature from Miguel. Jon, who consistently found himself missing deadlines or just barely meeting them, was sorry to interrupt but was sure Miguel and I would understand. After all, this was *urgent*. Miguel knew about Jon's constant state of urgency and decided it was time to send him a message. He looked him right in the eye and said, "Your failure to plan does not create an emergency for me. Please make an appointment."

I have thought often of that phrase and Miguel's choice. He not only attended to the project that was a priority for the organization but he taught someone an important lesson at a critical stage in his developing career. Too often, we are swept up in someone else's emergency. In truth, we might even be teaching people around us that it's okay to sweep us up. This is particularly true when we are part of a service organization or department. We pride ourselves on being always available, able to pitch in at a moment's notice. That's a great attitude, but in our quest to provide exceptional service, are we sabotaging our ability to attend to the real priorities of the organization while also enabling others to consistently make their lack of planning our emergency? It's good to be a team player and be willing to drop everything to help when there is a truly urgent matter. On the other hand, when you notice that most days are filled with "crises" that need your attention immediately, it is a good time to stop and ask if changes should be made.

OUR CALENDARS ALSO can become cluttered as a result of our own storytelling. For example, we fall victim to the thinking mind that nudges us to go to every meeting so we don't miss something that might advance our career, or lose a chance to be seen by the top management. We compose stories in our heads about how our presence will be missed or we might be seen as not fully engaged with the organization if we don't attend. Maybe those stories are true, and maybe they are myths derived from our fear or anxiety.

Whatever the reasons, most of our days are not spent addressing those things that are most important even though those things are never far from our minds. As we rush about attending to the urgent, we feel the need to attend to what is important and we bear the weight of that internal conflict.

For many of us, this conflict is often the source of the realization that even though our days are so busy that we fall into bed exhausted each evening, we have not focused on what we know is most important: the strategic plan, the breakthrough innovation we need to develop, the employee who needs support and coaching, our personal lives, or our own well-being. We look at our day packed with meetings and, alongside it, our list of responsibilities and it seems like something is wrong. We need to find a way to meet the day effectively, not let it "get away" from us, as Carey noticed.

And we might find it useful to explore a few other features about how we spend our days.

RESEARCH ON HOW WE SPEND OUR DAYS

As any group implementing new training curricula would, we wondered if we could see some of the effects of mindful leadership training in the workplace. With the help of some behavior researchers, we developed a nineteen-question survey and distributed it to seventy-two employees. These employees, representing all levels in an organization, were enrolled in the Institute's Mindful Leadership and Wellness course. They responded to the survey two weeks before class started and again two weeks after the course ended. The survey presented statements about the work experience and asked respondents to rate their experience of the statements on a six-point scale from Almost Always to Almost Never (see tables below). Their responses not only provide us with information about the effects of the training, but they also tell us something about the realities of working in today's world, and the effects of the internal battle between urgent and important.

"I AM ABLE TO MAKE TIME ON MOST DAYS TO PRIORITIZE MY WORK."

Rating	Pre-Course %	Post-Course %
1-Almost Always	6	13
2-Very Frequently	14	42
3-Somewhat Frequently	28	30
4-Somewhat Infrequently	28	11
5-Very Infrequently	19	4
6-Never	6	0

Perhaps not surprisingly, only a very small percentage of employees prioritize their work on a regular basis. Despite the fact that we know prioritizing may help us actually find the space to address the important, most of us don't do it. Perhaps we are running so fast in our overscheduled lives that we believe we simply cannot stop long enough to prioritize. Or perhaps we believe that if we just keep running, eventually we'll catch up and have time for everything. How's that working?

We also see from this first table the rather dramatic shift after just seven weeks of mindful leadership training. The environment the employees were working in did not change. Yet somehow we see the responses change from 20 percent of employees saying that they "almost always" or "very frequently" take time to prioritize their work before the course to 55 percent of employees choosing to make the time to do so after the course. It should be noted that the course curriculum includes a calendar exercise, which applies mindful leadership training to the scheduling of your day. This exercise, described later in this chapter, often helps people look more carefully at how they are spending their days, But the first step is to begin to question the assumption that you are not able to make the time to prioritize what is important.

"I AM ABLE TO MAKE TIME ON MOST DAYS TO ELIMINATE SOME TASKS/MEETINGS WITH LIMITED PRODUCTIVITY VALUE."

Rating	Pre-Course %	Post-Course %
1-Almost Always	3	13
2-Very Frequently	6	30
3-Somewhat Frequently	39	38
4-Somewhat Infrequently	26	15
5-Very Infrequently	22	4
6-Never	4	0

The emphasis on productivity in the business world has never been more acute. With global competition comes the need to use each moment wisely. Yet in our survey only 9 percent of employees reported "almost always" or "very frequently" making time to eliminate meetings or tasks that have limited productivity value—and remember, this was a survey of people in an organization consistently recognized as one of the best. Most of us know we're wasting valuable time, but we don't make conscious choices and push back on attending meetings or completing tasks when there is a better, more efficient way to do our work.

It is true that you don't always have the luxury of saying no to a meeting or a request, but when you honestly look at your day, is it also true that you can't make any changes, or at least suggestions, to lessen the waste? In my experience, if you question the status quo and make a thoughtful suggestion that has the effect of freeing up time for everyone involved, people generally meet your suggestion with enormous gratitude.

Wouldn't taking a few minutes to look for alternatives to meetings or tasks with little value provide returns that would more than make up for the time it takes to look at your day with a critical eye and make some conscious choices and creative suggestions? Before deciding that it won't work, take a look at the post-course numbers in this table. After just seven weeks, the 9 percent who were cutting down wasted time rose to 43 percent, and, just as importantly, the 26 percent who answered "very infrequently" or "never" dropped to just 4 percent.

"I AM ABLE TO BE FULLY ATTENTIVE IN MEETINGS, CONFERENCE CALLS, AND PRESENTATIONS."

Rating	Pre-Course %	Post-Course %
1-Almost Always	6	13
2-Very Frequently	25	62
3-Somewhat Frequently	42	21
4-Somewhat Infrequently	21	4
5-Very Infrequently	6	0
6-Never	1	0

What do we know about how we experience those meetings and calls that fill our calendar? We know we don't pay attention very well. In fact, only 31 percent of the employees in the study believed they were capable of being fully attentive in meetings most of the time (top two rows in the table). For the rest of the employees, it was pretty hit or miss. We realize that our minds are constantly being pulled away from the present moment, including those moments when we are trying to pay attention to a speaker at a meeting or an important phone call. Imagine the productivity gain if everyone sitting in the meeting was *actually in* the meeting. It *is* possible. In fact, in a relatively short period of time, mindful communication training moved responses in the top two rows from 31 percent to 75 percent.

"I AM ABLE TO NOTICE WHEN MY ATTENTION HAS BEEN PULLED AWAY AND REDIRECT IT TO THE PRESENT."

Rating	Pre-Course %	Post-Course %
1-Almost Always	4	26
2-Very Frequently	25	51
3-Somewhat Frequently	50	23
4-Somewhat Infrequently	11	0
5-Very Infrequently	8	0
6-Never	1	0

How can there be such a dramatic change in what people notice about their ability to stay attentive in meetings and on calls or working at the computer? This table answers that question and reflects the impact of the foundational training of mindful leadership to cultivate our ability to focus. Participants saw that their minds became distracted, and they were able to redirect their attention back to the present moment. The before-and-after responses in the top two rows for this survey question are virtually identical to those for the previous question. The practice of redirecting our attention when it wanders away from the sensations of the breath in daily meditation practice, for example, allows us to notice when the mind wanders from the present moment in any situation and redirect it back to the matter at hand. This capacity to focus our attention and refocus it when thoughts carry us away increases our ability to be present in our lives.

"IT SEEMS I AM RUNNING ON AUTOMATIC, WITHOUT MUCH AWARENESS OF WHAT I AM DOING."

Rating	Pre-Course %	Post-Course %
1-Almost Always	6	0
2-Very Frequently	29	8
3-Somewhat Frequently	22	11
4-Somewhat Infrequently	28	53
5-Very Infrequently	11	25
6-Never	4	4

These responses are perhaps the most troubling and revealing in the survey. We have a feeling that our days sometimes get away from us, as Carey put it, and when these seventy-two employees stopped long enough to reflect and respond to this question, more than one third believed that they were going through the motions, "without much awareness" of what they were doing most of the time!

Yikes! Is it any wonder that we're overtaken by the urgent and don't stop long enough to attend carefully to the important? Just imagine the impact this has on our ability to be creative, see clearly, and be compassionate. We need to find a way to spend our days aligned with what we know is important.

So let's take a look at how a mindful leadership reflection can help you take back your calendar and support your intention to attend to what is important rather than constantly chase what is urgent.

CALENDAR REFLECTION

In this reflection, you will once again explore meditation practices using body sensations, thoughts, and emotions as the objects of attention. You will also need a written or printed copy of a typical day from your calendar.

1. Take a comfortable seated posture, allowing your body to become still and to feel supported. As you are ready, bring your attention to the sensations in the body, including the sensations of the breath. Notice when your mind is pulled away, or drifts away, and redirect your attention to the sensations in the body. Practice with the body sensations as the object of attention for a few minutes.

2. Begin to slowly read your calendar page as though you have never seen it before, one entry at a time, paying close attention to the sensations arising in the body, as well as any accompanying thoughts or emotions. Be open and curious about what you are noticing. Notice if your mind becomes entangled in problem solving or judging a meeting on the calendar, and let that go, returning to slowly reading through the appointments and tasks on the page.

3. Are the sensations, thoughts, and emotions familiar to you? What else do you know about them? It can be helpful to write a list of what you noticed during this reflection. Try to use this reflection as a purposeful pause each morning for a couple of weeks. How has your list changed? Stayed the same?

The calendar reflection is a way to learn something about yourself and how you spend your day. The language of your body often begins to reveal something about certain meetings and something about your day in general. Did you notice a tightening in your neck as you saw that weekly update? Or a queasiness in your stomach when you noticed that deadline? Perhaps you noticed tightening in your chest when you saw your mile-long task list alongside your packed daily calendar.

Or, as is often the case, perhaps you noticed a feeling of tiredness overtaking you. When you stop to look at the intensity and speed of your day, just reading through the list of appointments can set off a powerful wave of fatigue.

What is your body telling you? Be curious. Begin to question the status quo that may have left you believing that there is no alternative to a calendar filled with meeting after meeting, and no time to prioritize or make conscious choices about scheduling time for the important items on the to-do list. Is the schedule that is often created for us by a variety of other people carved in stone?

By following this practice, you can become more intentional in your choices. What is the best use of your time? Why are you attending so many meetings? Are the right people gathering in the right type of meeting? Where is the space in the day for yourself?

Here are a few observations leaders have made about their calendars after exploring this reflection with the Institute in retreats and workshops:

> *There are so many meetings because I work in a culture that is so competitive that there is a sense that constant visibility is necessary to ensure advancement.*
> *I work in a culture where everyone needs to know everything. I wonder why?*
> *My calendar is packed with meetings where two or three members from my department attend because there is an inefficient matrix organization and a lack of trust.*

*I say yes to meetings simply because I am still too mired in
the details when I need to spend more time on the strategic plans.*

*My organization believes in meetings before the meetings,
and hallway meetings before that!*

*My calendar is so packed that I have no time to eat lunch.
No wonder I have headaches every afternoon.*

*Fifty thousand employees have the ability to put something
on my calendar and one doesn't—me!*

*The most important things are never on my calendar. This
is true at work and at home!*

*I am in the midst of a critical project and four meetings are
about it today but not one will move the project forward.*

*I need to let go of my thought that my career depends on
showing up to every meeting.*

The calendar reflection also raises questions about making
room for the teams you lead to grow, about the barriers to innovation that arise from a simple lack of space in the day, and about
the allure of reacting to situations simply to get something off the
to-do list. These and many other discoveries all begin with the
simple act of purposefully pausing for a few moments each day.
Using your body sensations to guide the way as you carefully take
in the information on your calendar, you honestly ask yourself:
Do I need to make changes to be more productive today? More
strategic? More compassionate?

As you read through your calendar, do you notice frustration,
anxiety, or anger? Ask yourself if you need to make changes to
the day's priorities to meet those emotions with clarity, creativity,
and compassion. Do you notice a thought like "There is nothing I
can do" arising? Is that true?

As this purposeful pause becomes a part of your mindful leadership exploration, you might notice a day when you feel very at
ease with the calendar content. What is different about that day?

Is it a day that is fully aligned with your leadership principles? Is it a day that reminded you that we are all connected, perhaps with some community involvement? Does it have a block of time dedicated to something that fuels your passion, the reason you decided to do the work you do in the first place? Is it taking care of the important matters? Is there anything you can do to replicate this type of day more frequently?

Rosalyn, a marketing director at a large, successful company, compared two back-to-back days from her calendar. Both days were similarly filled with meetings and calls. The only difference was that the second day began a half hour later than normal because she had blocked the time to see her son off to his first day of kindergarten.

At first, Rosalyn was confused by the differences she felt in her body as she looked at the two days. The first day's meetings almost instantly created tightness in her neck and a cascade of thoughts about deadlines she had to meet. The second day, the sensations were barely noticeable. In fact, she felt a lightness to the day. As she reflected on her experience, she finally came upon the explanation:

> When I originally blocked the time on my calendar to see my son off to kindergarten, I thought I was doing it for him. He would want me to be there and help him get on the bus and wave good-bye. All of which is true. But he is my youngest child, my baby, and I realize now that I was not blocking that time for him. I was blocking that time for me. And I can't remember the last time that I put something on my calendar that was for me.

Rosalyn discovered that scheduling some space for ourselves nourishes us in deep ways and can make our experience of the day very different. Scheduling space for ourselves is not a selfish act. In fact, finding ways to nourish ourselves and attend to our needs often requires that we *put it on the calendar* because we all know that if it isn't on the calendar, it doesn't happen.

Making choices about your calendar takes discipline and a strong commitment, but it need not happen all at once. A small change can make the day feel more spacious and can leave room for you to work on what is important. Begin with one step. At the end of your daily purposeful pause reflection, identify just one item on the calendar that you will choose to change so you can move toward the spaciousness you need to work on what is important. Or identify just one suggestion or best practice you want to explore with your colleagues to eliminate a task or meeting from your calendar. Can you imagine how welcome such a suggestion would be to you if someone found a way to give you some free time?

This reflection takes only a few minutes at the beginning of the day, but it has the potential to make the difference between autopilot leadership and leading with excellence.

PART 3

Realizing Your Full Capabilities as a Leader

CHAPTER 11

Leading Through Inspiration, Not Expectation

If your actions inspire others to dream more, learn more, do more and become more, you are a leader.

JOHN QUINCY ADAMS

HOW DO YOU INSPIRE PEOPLE WHOSE job it is to make a box of Chex cereal or Betty Crocker cake mix? After all, they're just two brands among hundreds you find in a grocery store. While it may be a good job, is there a way for a leader to inspire the wide range of employees charged with getting these products from a railcar of grain to your pantry? And why should it matter? Isn't it enough to tell employees the annual numbers your organization will need to hit for everyone to remain employed and get an annual raise or bonus? In other words, is it enough to lead by setting expectations of performance?

Is there anything to be gained by leading through inspiration?

A great deal. People thrive on what inspires them, not merely what is expected of them. What is expected of us is mostly what can be measured. It's black and white. You either do it or you fail to do it. Being inspired brings your authentic self into the picture, as well as your values and your principles, and it usually raises in you an appreciation of our shared humanity. Mindful leadership training can help us draw out and discover the deeper inspirations that drive us, and we, in turn, can inspire others with our passion.

Being inspirational is important for your day-to-day leadership, and inspirational leadership is particularly important when things are difficult. What can help you to be inspiring when things are tough? When people are feeling insecure and looking to you for leadership? Can reaching outside of your organization to the community you live in be a source of inspiration? In this chapter, we will look at these questions and consider a few examples that illustrate inspiring leadership.

IMPROVING THE LIVES OF CHILDREN— AND THEIR PARENTS

For the leaders responsible for Chex cereal and Betty Crocker cake mixes, inspiration came in the form of emotion-filled letters and blog posts asking the company, General Mills, to introduce gluten-free cereals and cake mixes. For the most part, parents wrote these letters. Children with a gluten intolerance cannot eat products made with certain grains, so most mainstream cereals are off-limits. Off-limits as well are many childhood treats like cookies and birthday cakes. Can you imagine being a seven-year-old who can't have a birthday cake like other kids, or who can't share in the special days at school by bringing in cupcakes or brownies?

A small group of employees began to look into the requests and the potential market for a new product line. They were people who were touched by the letters and who understood the need to help parents lessen the stigma these children felt as a result of being different. They wanted to see if there was a way to help. Eventually, they created a compelling business case to launch the company's first gluten-free product line, Chex cereals. The response from the employees involved with the new product line was incredibly positive, not because these were the most successful products being sold by the company but because they touched consumers in a very special way.

One parent wrote to the company and recounted to us that the morning her nine-year-old came down to breakfast to find a box of Chex cereal on the table, he thought it was for his sister. When his mother poured a bowl of it for him, he still didn't believe it and asked if this was really his breakfast. When she said yes, his face lit up as she heard him say, "Just like all the other kids." This letter and many like it were shared with the employees and talked about in the hallways and meeting rooms of General Mills. Making a difference in the everyday lives of others gave special meaning to the work. The employees who championed these products and the many products that would follow—Chex was soon joined by Betty Crocker gluten-free desserts—were inspiring leaders to all those who worked to bring the cereals and desserts to market.

People need to know what is expected of them in the workplace and the goals that must be met to keep the organization in existence. They may need to know, for example, the financial and sales needs of an organization. But that isn't enough if you want an organization with fully engaged employees, which is where inspiration comes in. Wouldn't you rather get out of bed in the morning because you feel inspired? Is there any doubt that when someone needs to choose to go the extra mile for the organization, he or she is more likely to do so with the image of the little boy sitting at his breakfast table, or perhaps eating his first chocolate birthday cake, than a year-end sales number in a chart? We are inspired because we identify with the parents' struggles. We might have encountered similar struggles in our own families or those of our friends. We feel good about our ability to make a little boy's life a little better. In this example, inspiration came from finding a bigger purpose for the work that the team was doing, a purpose that went far beyond the sales numbers needed for the investor report.

Of course, not everyone contributes to an organization that provides social services or produces products that will help a child, so how else can leaders inspire employees? What would make you feel inspired to go to work every day? Rather than immediately making a list of what you think might inspire you, try taking a purposeful pause for a reflection on inspiration.

REFLECTION ON INSPIRATION

Take a comfortable seated posture with your feet flat on the ground and your hands in your lap. Allow your eyes to gently close, and begin to practice by noticing your breath and other body sensations. As the body and mind begin to settle, ask yourself the following questions:

> When was the last time I felt inspired to contribute in some way? What was it about the project that inspired me to be committed to its creation or success?
> How does it make me feel right now as I call it to mind?

Remember that when you practice with a reflection, you may want to put aside the first one or two reflexive answers that arise and repeat the question again, being open and curious about whatever arises. Stay close to the sensations that may be arising as you ask the questions, particularly when you reflect on the way you feel right now as you call it to mind.

Take your time. Feel free to go back to practicing with your breath if you find yourself assessing or analyzing what arises. When the mind becomes more focused, repeat the questions again and see what arises.

For some of us, it has been a very long time since we felt inspired by something or someone. Don't limit yourself to the workplace when you are recalling the times you felt inspired. Perhaps there was a community project or other volunteer project that inspired you. Or perhaps you were inspired to take on a personal project by something you read or heard about.

When you are ready, open your eyes and spend some time writing about your responses. The act of writing can often help clarify and deepen the words and phrases that arise in a reflection. As you consider your list, ask yourself: What inspires me? Is it part of my work today? Is inspiration a part of my leadership?

When we are personally inspired, it is infectious. It is felt by those around us. When we are working for a paycheck, that is felt as well. If you no longer feel inspired, what is missing? Are there insights from the reflection that lead you to a new way to work that will kindle that inspiration in yourself and inspire those around you?

This reflection may take some time to unravel. Return to it every few days if it seems useful. There is no need to try to find an immediate answer. As you go through each day, you may begin to notice opportunities to make some changes to the *what* and *how* of your work that might begin to reignite the flame of inspiration.

INSPIRATION IN THE MIDST OF CRISIS

In the weeks immediately following the attack on the United States on September 11, 2001, all eyes were on New York City and its mayor, Rudy Giuliani. As he describes in his book *Leadership*, Mayor Giuliani had learned the importance of being there for the difficult times from his father. He learned that being present when people were in pain was the true measure of a person. His father's succinct way of putting it was "Weddings are discretionary; funerals are mandatory."

As mayor, Giuliani brought what he had learned from his father to bear on his leadership. He had a personal policy of attending the funeral of every person who died in the line of duty in New York City. After the attack on the World Trade Center, the sheer number of firefighters and police officers who lost their lives made adhering to that policy logistically impossible. In the days and weeks following the attack, there were scores of critical issues for the mayor to manage, including threats to security, environmental concerns, and the anxiety of an entire city. It certainly would have been understandable for him to let go of his policy in these extraordinary circumstances, and many on his team urged him to do so.

Instead, the mayor called his team together and told them that he or someone from his administration would attend every funeral for a New York City employee who died in the line of duty. He further instructed them that they were to do more than just show up. They were to speak with the family and "make their presence felt, speaking to and comforting the victim's survivors." It was critically important that their service was acknowledged and honored.

The choice Giuliani made was inspirational. Can you imagine its impact on his team? Wouldn't we all like to work with someone who so values and respects our contribution that employees are valued above all else? Can there be anything more inspirational than that? Throughout his leadership as mayor, Giuliani had prioritized the need to show up in the tough times and offer comfort. Even when the times got tough beyond what anyone could have imagined, his priority did not change. People were important. People came first. In your own leadership role, can you see ways to inspire those around you through simple gestures or honest communications that reflect their value, and the respect you have for each person? Leadership that understands that life can be challenging but that also remains committed to being there for the whole ride inspires people to give their best to the effort.

COMMUNITY SERVICE AS INSPIRATION: HOME DEPOT

One of the most effective ways for an organization to inspire its employees is through a community service project. When the organization is making a difference in the community, the employees often feel a collective pride in the efforts to give back and make a difference. They also feel connected to one another by a common goal to make our world a better place.

An example of an organization's powerful role in the community can be found in Home Depot's philanthropic project to help returning veterans. Its mission summarizes the commitment the organization and its employees made to the greater community:

> The Home Depot Foundation is committed to ensuring that every veteran has a safe place to call home—not just through financial donations, but also through the dedication and hands-on service of our store associates.

The company committed $50 million over three years to community housing projects. While this alone might have inspired some employees, the program added an important element that had even more potential to inspire. Home Depot's leaders directly involved its employees by inviting them to volunteer their services each year as part of their Celebration of Service program. The employees across the country responded. As a result, in 2011, the first year of the program, Home Depot volunteer employees completed more than four hundred housing projects for veterans. The program continues, partnering with local nonprofits dedicated to supporting the returning men and women who now need a little help. Who would not have a feeling of pride to be working with colleagues who not only contribute to the bottom line of the organization but also contribute to the community in such an important way? Talk about collectively making a difference!

In case you are wondering if size matters, it doesn't. Whether it is $50 million or $500, the hands-on involvement by the employees is much more likely to inspire than the organization writing a big check. Money can sometimes help make things happen more easily, but what touches most people's hearts, what makes them feel good about the work they are doing and the community they are a part of, is the feeling of connection. It is the feeling of being a part of making the world just a little bit better.

ARTIFICIAL INSPIRATION

It's especially important for us to remember that inspiration needs to be genuine. If the company says it encourages employee volunteerism but shows no support or recognition for the employees' efforts, the bad feelings engendered by this lip-service approach can backfire and make a work environment worse than if the company had chosen to do nothing at all. Few things are more de-motivating than artificial inspiration. So if you choose to experiment with a community project, be sure to back that up with financial support, or time set aside to execute the project well, and with appropriate communications to keep everyone informed. You may discover a little goes a long way toward helping the community and engaging your employees.

Artificial inspiration can also occur when leaders deliver empty speeches about the organization's financial picture and plans for the future. Diane, a financial vice president in a large medical device company, experienced the effects of artificial inspiration firsthand.

It had been a chaotic year, beginning with our company acquiring a very large competitor. As our two organizations integrated, there were so many distractions that our sales had dropped and we were being less innovative. We knew we would miss our quarterly projections. The share price had been declining a bit, and people were starting to question the direction we had taken.

Our president called a meeting of all the officers and directors to talk about the situation. We were anxious to hear what he had to say and quickly quieted down as he went to the front of the room. There was a kind of buzzing energy as we all waited to hear his assessment and plan for moving us forward.

He was very cheery and smiled from ear to ear as he spoke about the "little bump" we were experiencing and how we undoubtedly had the right plan to make our numbers next quarter. All we needed to do, according to his speech, was to be sure to "execute the strategy."

That was that. No specifics. No insights. No questions.

There was a palpable deflation in the room. It was as if the air had been drained and you could almost see people slumping in their chairs. Painting a rosy picture that did not even acknowledge the specific challenges didn't inspire us. Instead, we felt excluded and disrespected. We were seasoned businesspeople, and we knew we were experiencing more than a "little bump." This kind of pep talk does more harm than good. We left the room feeling even more concerned about the future of the company than we already were. Some people returned to their offices and dusted off their résumés.

Perhaps the president of Diane's company thought his role was to be a cheerleader. In fact, cheerleading in the workplace is what we call a "near enemy" when it comes to inspiration. A "near enemy" is something that looks much like the thing we're going for but is very nearly its opposite. For example, the near enemy of genuine empathy is pity, feeling sorry for someone, which is disempowering. So cheerleading and pep talking are indeed near enemies of true inspiration.

Corporate cheerleaders are robotic. They simply keep up the positive chatter no matter what the score is. They repeat stock phrases and try to pump up the employees' energy through reassuring words. The reality is that cheerleaders have virtually no positive effect and, as we saw in Diane's story, quite often have a significant detrimental effect. To be inspiring, you need to begin by being honest and open.

THE LIMITATIONS OF EXPECTATIONS

Another common way we fail to lead with excellence is managing by expectation rather than leading through inspiration. When we lead with excellence, our primary responsibility is to inspire those around us, knowing that if a capable employee is genuinely motivated, and he or she understands the ultimate goals, there is no need to micromanage. In fact, micromanaging more often than not simply prevents individuals and teams from reaching their full potential and inhibits innovation. When you are too prescriptive, you can impede the development of the independent thinking and experimentation the organization may need to push past set expectations and break free of the pack.

Natalie was a highly regarded director of a large electronics company. She had been on a fast track all of her career and had successfully solved some of the organization's stickiest challenges. She led a great team of professionals and enjoyed her role as a problem solver. One morning, she gathered her team and described a quality issue that had just arisen with an overseas supplier. She noticed her thoughts already recalling the steps used five years earlier when a similar situation had arisen. This time, though, she decided on a different approach. She had been wondering if sharing her past experiences to solve today's problems might sometimes be limiting the growth of her team, and perhaps the company.

So, rather than give her team the expectation that the shortfall in quality be handled in a way that she dictated, she turned the matter over to her team and listened to the ideas that arose. In a short time, they had identified a very different solution from what she had originally imagined based on her experience. Her smile brightened as she told me that "they had a faster, more efficient way to handle the immediate issue and, as a bonus, they developed a new safeguard to prevent the quality issue from happening in the future." Following Natalie's steps from five years ago probably would have taken care of the problem again this time—but by simply identifying the issue and then intentionally staying quiet, she ended up with a better result, and a more empowered team.

There are certainly times when we need to set expectations based on our learning and experience. We can't afford to reinvent the wheel for every project and decision. On the other hand, when we lead by setting expectations or by being prescriptive about what, how, when, and where, we can seriously limit innovation, and end up with an organization of disengaged employees.

Finding What We Expect to Find

Expectations can also be blinders that hinder our own capacity to see clearly. When we expect a result, we will often just look for information that confirms it, missing what is actually there. In a training session I was conducting, Lewis, a consumer insights researcher who conducted focus groups, provided a potent example of this principle.

We were working on mindful communication, noticing when the mind is distracted from taking in what our partner is saying. Lewis had been especially touched by the experience of openly listening without any expectations about what should be said. "Our work would be so much more accurate," he told me, "if we used this practice in focus group observations or consumer interviews. Instead, we sit behind two-way glass, waiting for someone in the consumer group to say what we expect them to say. Ten other people may have said completely contrary things, but the client or our manager expects his or her judgment to be endorsed, so we wait for someone to say what we are listening for."

Lewis may have been exaggerating slightly for effect, but think about how often you *do* carry expectations of a meeting into a conference room or a conversation. I have certainly found that when I go into a conversation or a meeting with a certain expectation of the outcome, I limit what I will discover and learn. Breakthrough ideas and exceptional achievement are easily limited by checking the boxes on a list of expectations, and true communication is limited by listening for the words we expect to hear.

INSPIRATION REQUIRES LEADERSHIP presence. It requires you to see what is here now rather than what you expect. This means you need to acknowledge failure and use it as a way to learn. It requires you to be readily able to let go of the way you did it last time, or how you "know" it will work. You need to be courageous enough to open to what arises in collaboration with others. You need to see when, in your attempt to be efficient by setting clear expectations about what needs to be done and how, you inhibit the growth of others and limit their potential to see new and better ways to move forward.

You need to seek and strike a balance. You need to set a direction and ensure that you share enough information to effectively engage people in their work. You also need to inspire and allow those you work with to collectively stretch as far as they can. When you're on autopilot, rushing from meeting to meeting, you are much more likely to manage by checklist, and accidentally treat those you are leading as order-takers. You are leading by rote, rather than leading with excellence.

You can use the following practice at the beginning of each day to help you more consistently find that balance.

PURPOSEFUL PAUSE: LETTING GO OF EXPECTATIONS

This purposeful pause builds on the calendar exercise in Chapter 10 and invites you to pay attention to the thoughts and emotions that may arise as you take a few moments to really look at the substance of some of your day's meetings.

At the beginning of the next workday, open your calendar and slowly read through the day's appointments. Feel your feet grounded to the floor and the breath sensations in your body as you ask yourself this question:

What might I discover if I went into my meetings without any expectations about how the issue should be resolved or the project should be accomplished, and instead went with the intention to listen carefully and to be open to whatever arises?

Ask yourself this question about each of the meetings on your calendar. Pay attention to the body sensations, thoughts, and emotions that arise as responses emerge. Perhaps you notice some uneasiness with the idea of letting go of taking the lead in the conversation as you have in the past. Where does the uneasiness come from—past experience or your imagination? Or you may notice emerging thoughts that warn of impending disaster if you don't just tell the team what to do next. Are such thoughts true?

As you walk to the meeting, or in preparation for appointments in your office, take a few moments to remind yourself of your intention to explore this purposeful pause, perhaps using the breath sensations or the sensations of your feet in contact with the floor as a reminder to deeply listen, to be open, and to let go of expectations. While you are in the meeting, notice when the urge to jump into the conversation to give directions arises, and ask yourself if that is the best choice right now. What happens if you stay quiet a little longer?

> If you make the choice to stay quiet, how does that feel in your body? Are you noticing emotions arising? What thoughts are arising? What do they tell you about how you are engaging with this meeting?

When they take this approach to meetings, many leaders report that at first their change in behavior surprises their teams and colleagues. Rather than quickly moving into the planning and execution stage, taking charge and assigning tasks, they become open and curious about new possibilities. What would happen in your team if the next time you began a new project, you *let go of expectations about it* and, for example, dedicated the first meeting to inviting creativity? Instead of announcing a typical meeting, where you would likely identify the parameters of the project and then divide up responsibilities, suppose you issued an invitation to find the best way to move forward, suggesting everyone give it some thought in advance of the meeting and bring in their best recommendation?

Isn't it possible that your meetings would change from a perfunctory passing along of information with due dates to a dynamic sharing of ideas and responsibilities? In short order, you may find that the new environment becomes a breeding ground for novel approaches and creative solutions.

Or what if you let go of the expectations you might have about a relationship that has historically been difficult? When you open up some room around what you "know" is going to happen, might you be able to shift the relationship, even just a little?

In her memoir *Madam Secretary*, former secretary of state Madeleine Albright offered an excellent example of the power of letting go of expectations. When she became the first woman to lead the State Department, she was committed to building a bipartisan foreign policy, which was particularly important for a Democratic administration sharing power with a Republican-majority

Congress. She would need Republican support for many of the priorities she wanted to accomplish, including participation in the Chemical Weapons Convention (CWC). The divide between the hawks and the doves had been deep in the past, and many expected she would make little headway.

Ignoring what history would lead her to expect, she began to reach out to influential Republicans, traveling to their home states with them to make personal appearances. These trips included one with Senator Jesse Helms of North Carolina, whom she feared might block a vote on the CWC. While in North Carolina, Albright presented Helms with a nightshirt that read "Someone at the State Department Loves You." They made a connection during their time together in North Carolina, and on the return flight Helms told Albright that he would not block the CWC vote.

Did they become best friends? Probably not, but letting go of an expectation that they would never see things the same way, or would always be so steeped in their party's politics that there was no room for independent thought, opened the door to a surprising ending.

CHAPTER 12

Not Just the Facts: The Role of Emotions in Leadership

I've learned that people will forget what you said, people will forget what you did, but people will never forget how you made them feel.

MAYA ANGELOU

IT IS COMFORTABLE FOR MANY OF us to live with the myth that we can turn off our emotions. In the workplace, and in other parts of our lives, we have often been conditioned to "control" our emotions, denying the critical role that they play. We learn to deny or push away the first hints of emotions we label as negative: fear, anger, sadness, insecurity. When things don't work out as we planned, or someone hurts us, we are trained to just box up those feelings, put on a happy face, and move on. Or we learn to distract ourselves from those emotions with drinking, eating, shopping, excessive exercise, or overwork. We learn to wear the masks of the business or professional world. In the process, we seal off an important part of who we are and so have an incomplete picture of how we are engaging with our world each day. We also ignore an important source of information about ourselves that is crucial to the understanding and full development of our leadership potential.

As a young attorney in a large Wall Street law firm, I certainly heard the "no emotions" message loud and clear. Keeping emotions under control and not letting anyone see you as an emotional being was a hard and fast expectation, especially for women. If I didn't learn how to hold back my emotions, I wouldn't be seen as a trusted adviser. Advice had to be rooted in facts and experience only. Emotions had no place in your deliberations and were likely to get in the way of making the best decisions. Or so I was taught . . .

Of course, as my experience as a lawyer grew and I found myself counseling clients on increasingly complex issues, I learned that combining my professional expertise with my emotional engagement enabled me to give the best possible advice, but it took many years and lots of practice to unlearn those early lessons about keeping emotions out of my work. That message does have an element of truth that must be acknowledged. We generally don't want to make choices when our state of mind has been overtaken by strong emotions. But trying to box up our emotions is an exercise in futility.

Mindful leadership practices can train you to notice your emotions and when your reactivity is triggered by an emotion. In this process, you are training your mind to notice *and* you are cultivating the space to make conscious choices. You learn that you can let go of futile attempts to suppress your emotions. You can expand your repertoire of responses to emotions, even those you label as the strongest negative emotions.

How?

Using the meditation with thoughts and emotions described in Chapter 9, you could go farther and deeper into experiencing and observing emotional content. As you identify a feeling as *anger*, for example, you might notice that the anger is not *you*. Nor do you need to go where the anger might want to take you.

You can experience the bodily sensations we associate with anger, you can notice thoughts that arise, but you don't need to *do* anything with the anger. You simply turn toward it, witness its presence, and feel it in the body. Some of what you begin to notice is that letting go of all the effort to deny and push away is a big relief!

You don't need to be afraid to acknowledge what is here. As you become curious about the anger, you may gain insight into the role anger has played in your life. With that knowledge, you may also see ways to make changes, or to be more patient or kind. The next step is to bring that practice into real-time choices in your life.

Robin was a hardworking physician who had recently been diagnosed with infertility. She was part of a close extended family. One sister had three daughters, and the other was pregnant. While on a mindful leadership retreat, Robin's emotions began to push to the surface.

> I came to realize that I was feeling anger, jealousy, sadness, and despair. I wanted it all to go away. I cried. I began to see that I had worked hard for a long time, filling my life with patients, committees, and teaching. Yet it still didn't feel like enough. The more I began to feel my emotions, the more I would add to my list. The more stressed I got, the more I exercised and told myself that I was doing self-care. It wasn't until I began to let down my guard and open to my true emotions that I could befriend them and learn from them. As I did, their grip on my life began to soften. It was okay to feel my anger and sadness when it arose, *and* I could still feel joy for my sister's pregnancy. They were not mutually exclusive. Giving myself permission to feel my emotions made me less likely to turn to distractions that were unhealthy. Meditation allowed me to see that ultimately, I was creating my own suffering by staying in this mode of constant striving in an attempt to distract myself from my own pain. Meditation allowed me to see another choice.

Robin was exhausting herself with her distractions, and she learned that such distractions were ineffective. Only when she allowed herself to notice her emotions could she begin to see clearly what was happening in her life. She could see how she was denying herself the joy of being an aunt, and she began to develop more self-compassion, which started to have a powerful healing effect. From this peaceful vantage point, Robin could make some decisions about how she wanted to live her life.

IT'S NOT ONLY the negative emotions that require our attention. We've equally been taught to blow past positive emotions, barely stopping to notice those moments that bring us joy or give us a sense of satisfaction. We are so busy moving on to the next goal that we fail to experience the joy or satisfaction of achieving the goal at hand.

The impact of failing to notice satisfaction or joy extends beyond us. It affects our colleagues. When we don't pause to appropriately acknowledge the fruits of others' hard work, for example, we foster a culture where a quick second or two to say "We did it" is thought to suffice for genuine acknowledgment. Why would we deny ourselves the shared experience of feeling good about the work we've done?

Similarly, we become so accustomed to being in a state of continuous partial attention that the moments that we could experience as pleasant or sources of happiness barely register: a daughter's smile; the warm, rich taste of coffee; the brilliant stars in the night sky.

Emotions make us human. They make us something more than computational devices. They allow us to feel connected to ourselves, to those around us, and to the world at large. They guide our choices, and they are often the source of our wisdom when there is no more data to gather, no one else to speak with, and no clear answer.

When the most prevalent message we receive about our emotions is that we should learn to box them up or not pause to fully enjoy the sublime moments in our lives, we are not cultivating this rich part of our humanity.

The meditation practice with emotions we have been exploring, beginning in Chapter 9, can help you experience your emotions simply, as part of your experience of this moment, so that you don't feel the need to push them away or change them. As you may have noticed, you have a wonderful ally in the journey to identifying and understanding your emotions and how they influence the way you lead.

Your body.

You feel emotions in your body long before you understand them cognitively.

When you notice bodily sensations like warmth in your face, a clenched jaw, butterflies in your stomach, or stiffness in your neck, you can use this information to help you recognize the emotions you're experiencing in any given moment. That's the first and most important step to developing an open, accepting, and curious relationship to your emotions. You begin to recognize them as vital parts of who you are. As you become more familiar with the sensations that accompany a strong emotion, you can learn to use those sensations as a form of early warning system. This practice can be richly rewarding but also quite challenging at first, as Mark, a veteran engineer, described to me.

I had lost touch with myself and struggled to notice any body sensations associated with my emotions. It was disheartening, as I would see myself reacting to my emotions in ways that were not healthy. About four weeks ago, I was in a meeting that was deteriorating quickly. As it unraveled, I felt a tightening in my chest. Finally I noticed! I was feeling angry, and I knew that when I am angry, I can get sarcastic, which never helps the situation. I brought my full attention to the breath in my chest until this dissipated and I felt more relaxed. I was able to engage with the situation more easily and, I think, more effectively.

As you develop a meditation practice that sensitizes you to emotional content, you also become more familiar with how emotions influence your actions. As a result of suppressing your emotions less and taking the time to see them more clearly, you begin to detect the influence emotions have on your behavior. Perhaps you begin to notice that you become very short-tempered right after you feel the butterflies in your stomach. You might become aware that the butterflies appear when you're unsure about a situation, and this feeling of insecurity leads to the short temper. The next time you notice the butterflies, can you feel your temper rising and make a more skillful choice before you erupt?

Little by little, we can all begin to learn more about who we are, and how we behave. As we open ourselves to what is here, and stop expending energy pushing away or trying to deny what we're feeling, we find a bit of space in which we can intentionally choose our next step. We respond to the realities of our lives more consistently.

THE ROLE OF EMOTIONS IN YOUR ABILITY TO CONNECT TO OTHERS

Perhaps you're thinking that your emotions don't have a significant influence on your actions. Or maybe you think that they only influence your actions when you are very, very upset, so much so that you are incapable of making connections and all you want to do is be by yourself in a quiet place until you calm down.

In either case, think again.

Take a typical day. Overbooked and running through the list of the day's obligations, you move from one meeting to the next until somewhere in midafternoon you find yourself in an important meeting that doesn't go very well. You walk back to your office feeling upset and accompanied by a cascade of self-judging and angry thoughts. As you head to your desk, your cell phone rings, and you hear yourself snapping at your spouse, who simply is calling with a question about this evening's plans. As you hang up, you have a brief moment of feeling confused by the exchange, or perhaps even feeling bad that it happened. Just as quickly, you push down those feelings and are on to the next item on your to-do list.

What happened on that call? The feelings from that meeting that didn't go so well were strengthened and fed by the thinking mind as it judged and replayed what happened and how it could have been different. The emotions that arose from the disappointment of the meeting were further churned up and fed by a stream of thinking. When we are caught in that swirl, our ability to connect fully with others and respond respectfully is diminished.

On some level, you may know that your behavior on the phone was a mistake, but more often, if you're like most of us, you simply move on, leaving behind hurt feelings and certainly not fostering your connection with your spouse. Later, either because someone brings it to your attention or because you have some quiet time to recall what happened, you can see the impact of your reactivity, but you still may not have discovered how to lessen the likelihood of it happening again.

When you practice with emotions, you begin to notice them as they're arising, and you begin to notice how the judging mind, and the thinking mind, serve to prolong the emotional impact that inhibits you from making clear choices about your next interaction or behavior. You also begin to understand the conditioning, people, and events that trigger certain emotions and, in turn, lead us to distract ourselves mindlessly with food, obsessive work, e-mailing, social networking, exercise, alcohol . . . you name it.

In bringing meditation practice to your emotions, you learn to notice your emotions without creating a full-length feature film about them. You have more space around them, which allows you to make choices about how you will respond to the feelings coming from your heart.

THE ROLE OF EMOTIONS IN YOUR ABILITY TO CONNECT TO YOURSELF

As you pay closer attention to your emotions as they arise in your body, you may begin to better understand how you are meeting the moments in your life. You might begin to see, for example, the toll that a persistent state of anger or regret takes on your well-being and your ability to make clear decisions. You may begin to notice that carrying the weight of these emotions translates into a constant feeling of being tired. Rather than push the feelings away or distract yourself, you can begin to turn toward those feelings with compassion. Leaving aside the judging mind, you look at the source of those emotions with a gentle curiosity and a goal of knowing yourself a bit better so you can expand your responses to those emotions when they arise. You also begin to notice the simple pleasures in your life that you might have been missing. You notice the warmth and light of a summer day as you walk to your car after work, and for a few moments, you feel the corresponding joy in your heart.

Our emotions add fullness and beauty to our lives. They help us understand what it means to be alive in the present moment—a present moment that may include emotions like sadness, joy, grief, fear, contentment, peace, happiness, or anxiety. When we approach emotions with open curiosity, they also can often be sources of great wisdom—the kind of wisdom that helps us connect with our own suffering, or actually acknowledge for more than a second the people and events that led up to the feeling of joy you are experiencing in this moment. As we open ourselves to this language of the heart, we also open our hearts to others. The more familiar we are with our own emotions, the better able we are to understand the behaviors of others. Failing to understand our emotions cuts us off from our own depth, the depth of the heart. And who really believes we can live well without our heart?

Lennart, a systems analyst who had begun practicing meditation recently, wrote to me early one morning to describe his commute. It was a cold, February day, and he was on the interstate in Wisconsin heading to work. He turned off his radio to be in the silence of the morning, and as he rounded a bend, he found himself driving into the sunrise. "I was so struck by the way the beams of light seemed to bounce off the clouds and fracture into millions of tiny reflections," he said. "I found myself almost literally breathing in the beauty and noticing a warmth that spread across my chest. I was so grateful that I had been there for that moment, fully there, not partially distracted. It was a moment of peace that brought tears to my eyes."

Lennart didn't need to go somewhere or do something to find that special moment. All he needed was to be more fully connected to his own heart.

THE ROLE OF EMOTIONS IN INITIATING, OR WORKING WITH, CHANGE

As leaders, when we value our hearts as well as our minds, we bring more of our capabilities into every situation. This helps us to broaden the repertoire of responses and actions we might take. We might find that when we listen with our analytical minds *and* our wise hearts, we see more, and we are more inspired, more compassionate, and more able to find ways to make a difference in taking on some of the significant challenges in our workplace and in our world. Perhaps my favorite example of making a difference in our world came from a story that began with a cab ride. Sheri Schellhaass, a vice president for research and development at General Mills, was returning from a business trip. Tired and anxious to get home, she found a cab at the airport and gave the driver her address. She was about to close her eyes and rest for a few moments when the driver began to chat about the cold winter weather.

The driver explained that he had been born in Africa and so the snow and ice of Minnesota's winter were new; he was having some trouble adjusting to the cold. Sheri's hope for a quick nap was soon set aside as she found herself becoming very curious about how this young man found his way to the Midwest. As the conversation unfolded, Sheri learned that the cabdriver came from one of the poorest countries in Africa, Malawi. There was no future for him there. Food and water were scarce—as were employment and educational opportunities—so he worked for years with the sole purpose of escaping to America.

His stories about the children who were malnourished and dying because of the lack of food were graphic. No food was available for the children during the school day, and often they would eat only once or twice a week at home. Sheri was deeply touched by what she heard, and it stayed with her long after the cab ride.

Sheri was a food scientist and a leader in her organization, and she and her team would sometimes volunteer their time to pack grain-based meals for the nonprofit organization Feed My Starving Children (FMSC). Sheri began to wonder if she could find a way to bring the work of FMSC to Malawi. She had a plan to send a million meals to the children. It would take money to pay for the meals and the shipping costs, and it would take a small army of volunteers. Sheri was able to get the funding from the General Mills Foundation. Now, who would be willing to pack all those meals?

One Wednesday morning, Sheri held an open meeting for General Mills employees. She spoke about conditions in Malawi and the million-meal plan, and she asked for help. The way Sheri's heart had been touched by the plight of the children of Malawi shone through her presentation, and by the time she was done, there was no doubt she would get all the volunteers she needed. By Friday morning, the sign-up sheets were full.

This story doesn't end there, though. The connections with Malawi would continue to grow as others were drawn into the circle to help. These connections would lead to the building of schools, funding to dig wells and improve access to clean water, and the transfer of technology to develop new ways to preserve the food that could be grown there so it would be available during the months of drought and famine. Hundreds of people became involved, and thousands of lives were affected.

This all began because someone was touched by the story of a cabdriver, and had the courage to use her expertise and influence to follow her heart. The project blossomed and grew because many others wanted to be a part of it. That kind of spirit embodies leadership excellence. It gave clear benefit to the people of Malawi, which was its primary purpose. As a by-product, the cultures of the many businesses and nonprofit organizations that ultimately became involved were elevated, and people there became more compassionate in their outlook. The project also made people feel very proud of the work they were doing and proud of the organizations that supported their involvement. It also told the outside world—the investor community, the potential employees— something about the special kind of people who were running the organizations. It touched the emotions of all who were involved, and it reminded them that we are all—everyone on the planet—in this together.

The Malawi story is an example of an executive inspired by a connection made during a cab ride, who then trusted her expertise and her emotions to guide her as she began to initiate a project that would bring about an enormous positive change. Our emotions are important allies in helping us navigate or initiate smaller changes as well. As we become more familiar with them, we may begin to trust that the uneasiness we are feeling in a meeting might be telling us something more than what other people's words are conveying, and we may be better able to ask the right questions. Or when we notice the anxiety that tells us that the choice someone is presenting does not align with our leadership principles, we may be more inclined to stop and seek an alternative.

Your emotions can also help you be aware of times when the team is not fully in the boat when you are introducing new initiatives. Leaders know how destructive it can be when a team is not in sync with a change. People will say the right things in a public setting and then leave without the commitment needed for the change to be fully implemented. When you learn to trust the emotions that arise in such meetings, however subtly, you can listen for the uneasiness that may suggest you need to encourage more candid conversations.

Navigating the emotional landscape more precisely and skillfully takes practice. We have not been taught to befriend our emotions, to learn to see them as sources of information or as guideposts to better understand ourselves and connect more fully with the people we encounter. We also have not been taught how to notice when emotions are fueled by the thinking mind and so are hijacking our ability to see things clearly and make wise decisions.

As we learn to approach our emotions with more kindness and curiosity, we begin to notice those times when our emotions are growing out of proportion to an event because our thoughts or our conditioning is feeding them. We begin to notice when we are shoving emotions aside, or distracting ourselves from them, rather than using them to help us understand more about ourselves and the situation at hand. Finally, we begin to trust the information that is being offered to us as we use our emotions to guide our choices. We need to place as much value on our capacity to understand our emotions as we do on our capacity to educate our discursive, cognitive mind. Relying solely on our thoughts and experience is simply not enough in today's world. We need to bring all of our capabilities, including our understanding of emotions, to our lives and to our leadership.

CHAPTER 13

Compassion and Kindness in the Workplace

A human being is a part of the whole called by us universe, a part limited in time and space. He experiences himself, his thoughts and feelings as something separated from the rest—a kind of optical delusion of his consciousness.

ALBERT EINSTEIN

SEVERAL YEARS AGO, I WAS GIVING a presentation at a conference in Massachusetts. I had just begun to take some questions when a young man near the back of the room stood up. Without waiting for the microphone, he simply called out, "Okay, you've convinced me that this training of the mind is needed to improve focus and creativity, but won't it just allow certain leaders to be more successful at being selfish and greedy?" Although it was not a question I had prepared for, it was a reasonable concern if you were new to the notion of mindful leadership training. In fact, it's a question I've been asked several more times in the years since.

I took a moment to gather my thoughts and then explained that the work of training in mindful leadership cultivates four fundamentals of leadership excellence: focus, clarity, creativity, and compassion. By far the most transformative one, for an individual, for an organization, and for the community, is compassion.

In fact, in many of the examples we've seen already in this book, the most significant shifts arose as a result of a deeper understanding of our connections to one another. As Father Thomas Merton said, "The whole idea of compassion is based on a keen awareness of the interdependence of all these living beings, which are all part of one another, and all involved in one another."

Time and again, as your practice develops and you begin to see your life with more clarity, you may begin to choose to make changes that arise from newly discovered, or uncovered, compassion. You may recognize suffering within yourself and apply some self-compassion to alleviate it, or you may see and understand something about the environment you work in that does not support or include some of your colleagues. You may begin to see how your work can be done in a way that is less harmful to the environment, or more beneficial to the community.

Contrary to what my questioner might have thought, compassion is an integral part of mindful leadership. Authentic training in mindful leadership strengthens the unselfish, generous qualities we also need to truly lead, rather than merely manage or execute. Among the recent research studies that have demonstrated a link between meditation and compassion is a study from David DeSteno's lab at the Psychology Department at Northeastern University, which investigated whether mindfulness meditation would lead to observable increases in compassionate behavior. The 2013 study found that about 50 percent of those who took part in an eight-week meditation program got up and offered their seat to a person on crutches wincing in pain, while only 15 percent of nonmeditators did so.

Compassion is a powerful force. When you open yourself to it, it fuels your courage and informs your choices. It originates in your heart, and is guided by your mind. Its power is evident throughout history and in your own day-to-day life. When we look to those moments in history when people took a stand against injustice or aggression, their strength and courage to do so came from their compassion, from their deep and true understanding of the suffering that existed and the desire to do something about it. Examples include Abraham Lincoln, Martin Luther King, Mother Teresa, and Mahatma Gandhi. Their compassion led to their choice to take a stand and, in so doing, to offer acts of immeasurable kindness to those who were suffering. They exemplified powerful leadership presence.

In your own life, you may not be taking a historic stand on a large societal issue. Nevertheless, you can still notice that when you are deeply touched with an understanding about the suffering of others, you feel a pull to do something. As you become more aware of when you are distracted from paying attention to this tug on your heart, you are more able to deepen your understanding and choose an action that will alleviate the suffering. When this happens, the strength of your heart fuels your actions, and you feel unstoppable.

Not surprisingly, noticing our own suffering is the starting place for training ourselves to cultivate compassion. We are generally not very good at acknowledging the difficulties in our lives, but quite good at denying and ignoring those parts of our lives that are painful. This is especially true for leaders. I once heard a president of one of the best business schools in the world speak about the reluctance of MBA students to admit to others a failure or difficulty in their lives. In fact, he noted, the students were barely aware of their failures and difficulties. He concluded that "success is a great place to hide." Indeed, when we have parts of our lives that others tell us are going well, we can easily distract ourselves by placing all of our attention on those parts. We can choose to live a partial life, ignoring the reality that all the parts of ourselves taken together—not just the successful ones—make us who we are.

Success is not only a good place for MBA students to hide. Leaders who have been generally successful are also reluctant to acknowledge difficulties in their lives. After all, so many things are going right, why bother with those things that are causing pain? This is especially true when leaders are also caretakers. They spend all of their energy trying to fix things for their families, friends, colleagues, neighbors, and teams. Meanwhile, they ignore or deny their need to relieve their own pain, their need for self-compassion.

Matthew, a highly talented businessman at a major law firm, discovered the value of self-compassion.

On February 11, my brother-in-law died very tragically at the young age of thirty, leaving behind my sister, her ten-year-old daughter, and a baby on the way. My family is incredibly close, and this came as a complete shock. I flew down to Miami immediately to be with my sister.

In the rush of all the things that needed to be done, I just started "doing"—making the arrangements, working with the medical examiner, the funeral director, closing bank accounts etc. For two days, I just "did" and did not "feel." My brick wall went up and NOTHING was going to knock it down! I found that the consequences of this inattention, mindlessness, can be costly.

My stomach was in true knots. I was not sleeping. I couldn't eat. I gave up running (my passion) because I was so tired and strung out. I was ignoring really important cues. I was trying to stay focused on everyone else's needs. I wanted to "fix." Eventually, I could not ignore how I felt any longer.

I then remembered my mindfulness training. I got up in the mornings and did walking meditation for about thirty minutes. It was the best time I spent on myself. It moved me from autopilot to complete awareness of the present moment. I began seeing, hearing, smelling, tasting, and feeling the present moment. I felt the pain of loss, the anger at the situation my sister and family were in, the concern for my own children, and I cried.

I remembered to breathe. Such a simple thing, but it made all the difference. When things became overwhelming, I stopped, paused, and breathed. I then became a better brother, father, and son. I let everyone in and felt such deep comfort and even joy in the celebration of my brother-in-law's life. I was more responsive, more informed, and less robotic. I was also able to sleep and eat, which made the tasks and thinking at hand much more bearable.

I allowed myself to feel my life in the moment, and if I hadn't, I would have missed feeling the love and support from my friends, family, and co-workers. I would have missed knowing that people can be incredibly kind, amazingly generous, and are willing to help at a moment's notice. I would have missed the opportunity to remind myself that I am blessed.

My sister had her baby last week, and both she and the baby are doing well.

There are many lessons in Matthew's story. Can you see yourself acting in a similar way when you are in a crisis scenario—so intent on "fixing" that you lose sleep, eat poorly, and deny or ignore your own emotions? I certainly could for much of my life. What I learned was what Matthew so beautifully described. Being self-compassionate *does not* negate your ability to be helpful and supportive to others. You don't need to push your pain away so you can keep "fixing" things. In fact, your willingness to see your own situation more clearly enhances your ability to be more fully awake to those around you, what they need *from* you, and their support *for* you.

HOW DO YOU CULTIVATE COMPASSION?

Cultivating compassion often begins with a kindness practice that helps us to recognize and open our hearts to the fundamental needs of all human beings.

Let's look at a few of those needs:

We all want to feel safe from physical and emotional harm.
We all want to feel strong and healthy.
We all want to feel happy.
We all want to live with ease ("live with ease" as it is used in
    this meditation means to live with clarity and equanimity).

These four statements acknowledge the common wish we all have to lessen suffering in our lives. They form the basis for a meditation that can be used as part of your daily practice.

KINDNESS MEDITATION

To begin, follow the same four steps laid out in all of the meditation practices you have worked with.

Kindness Meditation Practice—Part One

▶ 1. Find a comfortable seated position, allowing your body to become still and feel supported.

2. Begin practicing with awareness of your breath. As you are ready, silently say each phrase below twice, taking your time to attend to your body, especially the area of your heart, as you say each one. Pause for a couple of breaths before moving on to the next phrase. The two objects of attention are (1) the experience of saying the phrases and (2) the body sensations that arise as you say the phrases.

"May I feel safe from physical and emotional harm."
"May I feel strong and healthy."
"May I feel happy."
"May I live with ease."

3. As you direct your attention to each phrase, bring an open curiosity to whatever body sensations you are noticing. You do not need to change or control or assess what you are noticing.

4. Notice when your attention is pulled away or drifts away and redirect your attention back to the two objects of attention in this compassion meditation—the phrases and body sensations. No need to judge how well you are doing with the practice.

It is important to understand that as you aspire to these states of being—safety, strength, happiness, and living with ease—you are not making a wish to feel these things when they are not true. "May I feel happy" is an aspiration; it is not a command to force yourself to feel happy and ignore your experience. This is not about cultivating delusion. Rather, it is a meditation that opens your heart and mind to these needs, reminds you of our shared humanity, and emphasizes the importance of *feeling* what is here.

What did you notice? How did it feel to be offering yourself self-compassion, kindness? At first, it may feel strange to do so. You might be unaccustomed to acknowledging your humanity in this way. Or it might raise strong feelings of loss as you recognize, perhaps for the first time that you, too, want to live this way. We all want to feel safe, strong, healthy, and happy. We all want to live our lives with ease, that is, with a deep sense of clarity about what is here and how we want to meet each moment as it arises.

You might also notice any emotions or thoughts that seem to be common visitors to your kindness practice. Does the practice sometimes generate feelings of discomfort? Are those feelings familiar? Do you notice a warmth or familiarity as you recognize your needs, and perhaps attend to yourself in a way that has been missing? Perhaps you notice feelings of guilt arising. Or thoughts like "This is selfish." Is that true?

Why would you believe that all human beings want these fundamental things to lessen the suffering in their lives but not acknowledge that wish for yourself? What is that about? Is the relief of suffering right for everyone else but not for you? Be gentle with yourself as you explore these questions. Stay with this practice for several days before moving on to the next part, or returning to the other daily meditations in this book. Be open and curious about whatever arises.

When you are ready, you can move on to part two of the Kindness Meditation Practice.

Kindness Meditation Practice— Part Two, Expanding the Circle

You can continue this practice by saying the phrases below, which direct the same wishes you made for yourself to others.

▶ First, choose someone who loves you unconditionally. This is a person in your life who loves you exactly as you are. It is helpful to call to mind an image of this person before beginning to silently repeat each phrase twice, pausing for a few breaths before moving on to the next new phrase.

"May you feel safe."
"May you feel strong and healthy."
"May you feel happy."
"May you live with ease."

What do you notice about the sensations that arise? Do you notice a feeling of warmth in the area of the heart? Or perhaps a lightness in the chest as you direct these phrases toward someone who loves you?

Are you aware of feeling connected to that person? After practicing with body sensations or your breath for some time, you are ready to continue to expand the circle you are beginning to create.

Taking your time, offer these same four phrases, in the same way that you have offered them to yourself and to someone who loves you, to the following list, one by one:

someone you love
a mentor or teacher
a dear friend
an acquaintance (someone you know but not very well)

Each time you choose someone new, remember to begin by bringing an image of the person to mind. When possible, allow a few minutes of practicing with body sensations or with the breath before focusing on a new person.

Finally, call to mind someone who is difficult in your life. Recognizing that he or she also just wants to feel safe, happy, healthy, and strong, and to live with ease, expand your circle once more by offering these four phrases to him or her. You don't need to engage in thinking about why this person is difficult, or the suffering you believe he or she has caused. Let go of judging. For now, simply acknowledge that this person shares these fundamental human characteristics with all of us.

Pay careful attention to what arises in your mind as you do this practice. What are you noticing? There is no right or wrong answer to these questions. If a cascade of thoughts—judgments, memories, stories—arises, notice that the thoughts are here, intentionally let them go for now, and then return your attention to the phrases and the sensations in the body.

Be gentle with yourself. If it is too difficult to offer these compassionate phrases to someone who has hurt you, try offering it for both of you at once. This practice does not require that you change anything—it does not require that you forgive anyone, or make modifications to how you feel about them. While you may notice over time that there may be a subtle, or not so subtle, shift in your feelings toward someone who has hurt you, that is not a goal of this practice. The kindness practice simply opens your heart in a way that acknowledges that all of us are in this world together, that there are fundamental human desires we all share, and that we all have suffering in our lives from time to time.

In the final moments of your meditation, return to part one of this practice, cultivating self-compassion by offering these four phrases to yourself.

This practice can help us understand the value of kindness, the action that comes from our efforts to embody compassion. Kindness meditation opens our hearts and can put us in touch with our own needs and the needs of others at a very fundamental level. It can also help us use kindness to befriend those needs and pay closer attention to them, and to the many ways we have been conditioned to deny or ignore them.

Former Secretary of State Colin Powell says kindness is "not just about being nice; it's about recognizing another human being who deserves care and respect." In his book *It Worked for Me*, he shares a wonderful little story about a discovery he made while secretary of state.

I slipped away one day from my beautiful office suite and vigilant security agents and snuck down to the garage. The garage is run by contract employees, most of them immigrants and minorities making only a few dollars above minimum wage.

The garage is too small for all the employees' cars. The challenge every morning is to pack them all in. The attendants' system is to stack cars one behind the other, so densely packed that there's no room to maneuver. Since number three can't get out until number one and two have left, the evening rush hour is chaos if the lead cars don't exit the garage on time. Inevitably a lot of impatient people have to stand around waiting their turn.

The attendants had never seen a Secretary wandering around the garage before; they thought I was lost . . . I asked about the job, where they were from, were there problems with carbon monoxide, and similar small talk . . . After a while I asked a question that had puzzled me: "When the cars come in every morning, how do you decide who ends up first to get out, and who ends up second and third?"

They gave each other knowing looks and little smiles. "Mr. Secretary," one of them said, "it kinda goes like this. When you drive in, if you lower the window, look out, smile, and you know our name, or you say 'Good morning, how are you?' or something like that, you're number one to get out. But if you just look straight ahead and don't show you even see us or that we are doing something for you, well, you are likely to be one of the last to get out."

This story is a great reminder of the sameness of humanity. We all are important. We all deserve respect. We all appreciate kindness.

COMPASSION AT WORK

Compassion can be brought into each workday through simple acts of kindness. When we choose to take a purposeful pause and offer a colleague a compliment or a word of encouragement, or inquire into the person's well-being, we bring kindness into the workplace. The ripple effect of kindness is limitless. A compassionate leader can transform the most challenging workplace. When a leader embodies compassion and is seen as a kind person, even his or her toughest messages are more likely to be received well. After all, when we work with someone who honestly respects, includes, and values us, it goes a long way to making us trust his or her decisions.

Being kind is not the same, however, as being polite or politically correct. Kindness comes from compassion, an authentic connection to others and the pains and joys they feel. If it does not come from the heart, it can have a disastrous effect. When someone we have a significant relationship with, like a boss or a colleague, is just going through the motions, asking "How are you?" but not really caring to stay around for an answer longer than "Fine," we notice the insincerity. When we encounter that person, aloof and disconnected, we don't feel respected, included, or valued. We feel invisible.

Compassion practice can also help us form a new relationship with those who are difficult for us. We begin to break through the walls that we sometimes build up around us when someone is difficult. We build those walls to protect ourselves from harm, but those walls also serve to keep us imprisoned, limiting our capacity to live life to the fullest.

Fabrice, a hardworking leader in the sales division of a multinational aerospace company, described to me his experience trying to change a relationship with a difficult boss. Fabrice was very good at his job and was well liked by his colleagues. Everything seemed to be heading in the right direction until a new manager, Steve, joined the organization and became Fabrice's boss. At first things seemed fine, but soon Steve began to micromanage Fabrice and undercut him by excluding him from important meetings. Despite several attempts to speak with Steve about these issues, nothing changed for Fabrice, and soon he found himself dreading every encounter with Steve.

Fabrice had been developing a mindful leadership meditation practice with purposeful pauses for the past few years, and had begun wondering if it might be helpful in his situation with his boss. One day, as he was sitting at his desk, the phone rang. He glanced up at the caller ID, and as he read Steve's name, he simultaneously noticed the tightening in his chest. Before he even picked up the phone, Fabrice could feel in his body that he was becoming defensive and closed, and he also realized that this could only make things worse. Steve wanted Fabrice to come to his office for an emergency meeting.

As he gathered his laptop, Fabrice decided to use a kindness meditation like the one described earlier as he walked to Steve's office. Every few steps, Fabrice would offer Steve a different phrase (e.g., May you feel strong and healthy), rotating through them and then beginning again. Later, Fabrice described what he noticed:

> Little by little, my body began to open, the tightness lessened, and my walk became more fluid. The closer I got to his office, the clearer I became that he wanted the basics of life, just like me. I arrived at the meeting without the defensiveness and anger that had been with me in recent weeks. As I sat across from his desk, our conversation was more productive than it had ever been. I suspect it surprised him, because as I was leaving, he thanked me for my contributions. That was a first, for him and for me.

Compassion opens the door to the connection between your mind and heart. At a time when many people think of the workplace as draining and impersonal, the need is greater than ever for each of us to cultivate and embody compassion. Fueled by the wisdom of your heart, compassion is the essential partner to your mind's analytical training. Heart and mind are deeply connected, and both are necessary for leadership excellence. As Pir Vilayat Inayat Khan, a great Sufi teacher of the twentieth century, once said, "The mind is the surface of the heart, and the heart is the depth of the mind."

CHAPTER 14

Seeing the Big Picture

You are not here merely to . . . make a living. You are here in order to enable the world to live more amply, with greater vision, with a finer spirit of hope and achievement. You are here to enrich the world, and you impoverish yourself if you forget the errand.

WOODROW WILSON

WHAT GETS IN THE WAY OF SEEING the big picture?

What *is* the big picture, anyway?

In your meditation practice and purposeful pauses, you probably have already begun to see the many ways in which you can prevent yourself from realizing your full potential because you are, at best, paying partial attention. In particular, you may have seen how your ability to focus, to see clearly what is here, and to find the room to be creative can be clouded by a hurried, over-scheduled existence. Your reflections have invited you to listen to your own principles, to become more familiar with your inner wisdom, and to bring compassion into all areas of your life.

As we train the mind's capabilities, we expand our repertoire of ways of meeting the chaos of our world. We begin to be more aware of our own ripple effect. With these new discoveries, we begin to see opportunities to make conscious choices that can change the status quo. These choices are fueled by our ability to stop and see beyond today's "crisis," beyond our next objective, beyond ourselves, and beyond the narrow focus of getting ahead. We more frequently are able to see the big picture and our role in it.

The potential changes that arise from this new big-picture view are limitless. The big-picture view can help us reorder our priorities so we more consistently attend to what is really important. For some, seeing the big picture translates into behavioral changes that deepen connections with colleagues and make the workplace or community more respectful and inclusive. For others, it is the impetus for cultivating a new work environment, one that recognizes the need for openness and flexibility as a precursor to breakthrough innovation. Sometimes the big-picture view drives us to take the time necessary to find win-win-win solutions: good for the organization, good for employees, and good for the community.

Often your ability to see the big picture can be fueled by stopping long enough to notice the costs of your current lifestyle. Sometimes that stopping is thrust upon you by a personal crisis that yanks you into the present and leaves you with a new perspective about the world and your role in it. Sometimes it comes from a choice you make to get away from it all for a while, to be in an environment that is not hurried and overscheduled. You might decide to go on a retreat, or spend some time in the quiet of the countryside. One such place to get away from it all is a sustainability education center in rural New York called Better Farm. Its manager, Nicole Caldwell, shared with me her observations about those who come to spend some time there:

> When people arrive, they're tied to their smartphones, their Facebook pages, and their television shows. They make phone calls incessantly: to check voicemails, to make sure X, Y, Z has been taken care of in their absence, to see if they are missing anything in the hour since they last called. Some can't hold conversations. The whole time, they're gripping their phone and checking for texts, Twitter updates, constantly interrupting

with "Let me show you this video" or "Oh—sorry, I have to take this call." It's amazing to see; this limited attention span and unwillingness to be in the moment with another human being. Time passes and they begin to live and work with others in the community that they are sharing in for a while. And the iPhones begin to take a less important role in defining their lives.

In a newfound connection to other human beings who actually share a living, working, and creative space, visitors relearn what it is to feel compassion and to laugh—not at something like a movie or an Internet meme, but to really laugh and experience joy in the presence of others. Suddenly, people who before never experienced silence can be found sitting still outside and just breathing, watching a bird flit from tree to tree, or simply petting a dog. They are realizing that that world of virtual communication that they access through social networks and their smartphones is not as interesting as the world that is right in front of them.

I witness a similar transformation as part of the mindful leadership retreats. Participants often experience the early practice sessions, where iPhones and laptops are banned, as addiction withdrawl. Yet by the time we reach the final day of the training, many have learned that too much is missed, and too much is lost, when we spend almost every minute of every day tied to virtual communication. The discovery of the small picture, the one that tells us about ourselves, is very often the best portal to understanding our obligation to see the big picture, and our capacity to affect it.

Nowhere was this discovery more poignantly expressed than one Saturday afternoon when George, the president of an apparel company, told the other members of the retreat what he experienced the evening before. At the end of the meditation session on Friday night, we had begun an extended period of silence that would end the next day. During the silence, there would be no TVs, no iPhones, no computers, and no talking.

As we dissolved the silence on Saturday afternoon and began to discuss our experiences of the extended silence, George was the first to speak.

> After each session since we began three days ago, the minute I walked out the door of this building and headed back to my room, I reached into my pocket to check my BlackBerry. But last night, before I came to the evening session, I knew we weren't supposed to use the electronics during the period of silence so I zipped it up in my suitcase. As I left the evening session, of course, my hand habitually reached into my pocket. The Black-Berry wasn't there, and at that moment, I remembered that Janice had said something about the night sky. So, I looked up and saw the incredible magnificence of thousands of stars. I was frozen to the spot as I realized that I hadn't seen the stars in twenty years. I lay down in the grass and took it all in. I can't tell you how long I stayed there, awestruck by the brilliance of the sky. Eventually I got up and went to bed, but when my alarm went off in the morning, the first thought in my mind was . . . what else have I missed while staring at my BlackBerry?

There was a deep stillness in the circle as each of us listened to George's story. It offered us an insight into the "small picture" that helps us keep in mind the "big picture." There is nothing wrong with iPhones or laptops or BlackBerrys. We need these devices to work in today's world—but when they take over our lives and we are no longer choosing to use them in a way that supports how we want to live, we lose part of ourselves, often the richest part of being human.

THE WORLD ECONOMIC FORUM

Although I have worked with leaders from all sectors of society who try to keep the big picture in mind even as they set their organization's immediate goals, nowhere is the desire to see the big picture and to influence it in a positive way more apparent than at the World Economic Forum. For one week each year the picturesque mountain town of Davos in southwestern Switzerland becomes a meeting place like no other as it welcomes this annual event. Influential people from every sector of the world community make the trip by plane, train, and bus to gather in the snowy Alps in January for several days of talking and making connections. It's a conversation about how to change the world.

In the halls of the Congress Center, and in meeting rooms in the town's hotels, groups gather to speak candidly about major issues and opportunities evolving in our world. In workshops and idea labs, at lunches and dinners, in the hallways and on the shuttle buses, these conversations and debates almost always occur out of range of the eyes and ears of the media. The fact that media are restricted to certain plenary sessions and participants are instructed not to attribute statements to people by name when they talk later about a session or conversation fosters candid interactions. It can also cultivate an environment where courageous leadership can flourish. It is an environment that reminds us of the big picture, the fact that we are all in this together.

Among the participants are prime ministers, kings, princesses, industry leaders, artists, social entrepreneurs, nonprofit leaders, musicians, academics, and scientists, as well as a group of selected young leaders whose alumni include Bill Clinton, Vladimir Putin, and Angela Merkel. I was honored to be invited to the 2013 meeting to share my work in one of the forum's workshops, and to guide a morning meditation session, the first ever offered at Davos.

Preparing for this workshop was a journey that will forever stay with me, as I came face-to-face with the old adage "Be careful what you wish for." On the one hand, there could be no greater opportunity to bring mindfulness training to leaders who could make a difference, who could have a very big ripple effect. On the other hand, I would be offering a workshop dedicated to mindful leadership at a time when mindfulness was known mainly as a training to reduce stress or manage health problems, but only beginning to be known as a critical mind training for leaders. It was entirely possible, perhaps probable, that training the mind to cultivate a leader's capability to focus, see clearly, be more creative, and embody compassion would be such an unusual idea that few would choose to attend. Even so, I knew that mindful leadership training was a critical piece of a person's development as a leader, so I was fully committed to the opportunity.

When the organizers asked me how I would like to offer the workshop, I quickly decided that it would be important to have enough time for multiple experiences of the mindful leadership training itself—not just an abstract overview. I didn't want to simply describe the mind training that cultivates focus, clarity, creativity, and compassion. I wanted to offer the opportunity to try it, and to engage in some dialogue. I also wanted a co-presenter who works directly with the neuroscience of mindfulness. Enter Professor Mark Williams, director of the Oxford Mindfulness Center and a professor of clinical psychology at the University of Oxford. I was honored to be co-presenting with Mark, an expert in his field and an all-around great person. While I spoke about mindful leadership training and workplace research, Mark shared some of the neuroscience research that explores how the mind's capacity for seeing clearly and for making good decisions can be adversely affected by the complexity of modern daily living, and how mindfulness training begins to develop our capacity to minimize those deleterious effects.

The Mindful Leadership Experience workshop was scheduled on the morning of the first day of the forum. Offering it early in the forum would allow those touched by the practice to participate in the morning meditation sessions scheduled in the subsequent days. Mark and I arrived early the morning of the workshop and helped the forum's staff set up a semicircle of about twenty-five chairs with some extras stacked against the wall.

Now all we needed to do was wait to see if anyone would show up.

The doors were finally opened, and a steady stream of people began to fill the semicircle. Soon every seat was taken, and the staff began to bring in more chairs. Eventually the room held nearly seventy people, and the staff had to close the session. We later would run into people who told us they were turned away at the door. So much for no one being interested in how to train the mind to cultivate the fundamentals of leadership excellence.

As the workshop began, I was struck by who was gathered before Mark and me. I looked into the faces of those who had come to explore something new and saw a definition of the big picture that I'd never understood so clearly before. Represented in the room was the very definition of diversity from every imaginable point of view—age, religion, race, ethnicity, gender, and more. These were people with backgrounds and responsibilities that spanned the spectrum of human endeavor, from artists to entrepreneurs to publishers, economists, and royalty. We were all there to learn about and experience mind training that would, among other things, teach us to feel, and to be, more connected—to our own wisdom, to those around us, and to the world in which we live and lead. Never had the universal appeal of mindful leadership training been more apparent. I found myself taking a moment to just breathe in the experience.

The workshop unfolded as I showed people the diagram that details the fundamentals of leadership excellence (see Chapter 3)—focus, clarity, creativity, and compassion. I spoke about the ways meditation practice and purposeful pauses cultivate and strengthen those fundamentals. Mark presented cognitive neuroscience research and spoke about the impact of a chaotic world on our ability to make the best decisions and to see things clearly. Then I spoke about how the Institute for Mindful Leadership has been bringing this training into organizations from all around the world.

Along the way we paused to practice meditation, we paused to explore a reflection on leadership excellence, and we paused to engage in open dialogue. The group was bright, warm, and curious. As with every group of leaders I have ever taught, the common challenges of leading in the twenty-first century soon became evident.

Among the most prevalent challenges participants identified was the recognition that we are overscheduled and constantly distracted, leaving no space for us to find the most skillful ways to guide, or to initiate, change. We multitask even though some part of us knows that so much is lost when we do so. Even when we get things done, we don't find the time and space to acknowledge the accomplishment, to debrief with our teams, and to learn from any mistakes. There is inadequate space to lead, not only in the way we want to lead, but in the way *we need to lead* to make a real difference in how we address the organizational and global challenges we face today.

The group was also touched by gaining some insight into the personal costs of so much distraction and busy-ness. When I told the story of a successful man who realized through his mindfulness practice that he had missed being present for most of his life, there was a deep silence in the room, and I noticed many people slowly nodding in recognition. We know that working very hard without really paying attention fully to what we are doing, and who we are doing it with, simply leaves us feeling empty.

When the workshop was over, many people stayed to speak to us personally about their experience. In fact, over the next four days, I would often have the opportunity to hear from people who attended the workshop, encountering them in the hallways or the dining room or another session. They shared with me their stories of incredible challenges and inspirational tales of groundbreaking leadership.

One young leader from Africa spoke with me about his hope of bringing mindfulness training to the new generation of leaders in his country, where a common belief was that every leader over the age of forty had been corrupted. The young people wanted a different kind of leadership. Another person spoke of her hope that this training would help to equalize the disparity in opportunities for women in her Middle Eastern country. A few people shared stories of the hardships in their organizations caused by the shaky economy, and the sadness they had felt when having to close factories and put people out of work. They wondered if mindful leadership training could have any impact on the events leading up to those decisions. Some people I spoke with had simply reached a point where they were tired and needed to find another way to deal with the complexity of their lives and the ever-increasing responsibilities of leadership.

One parent from the Middle East with an autistic child spoke of how there were no support services available to her. She wondered whether the training she would experience at a mindful leadership retreat, in addition to helping her, might teach her something that might help her child.

I was deeply touched by these conversations. Defying the common portrayal of leaders as only caring about the success of their organization, their next campaign, their public persona, or enriching their own net worth, here were people who wanted to be better at leadership so that they could make a difference. The mix of people was extraordinary, but there was a common motivation. They could see the big picture and they didn't like what they saw. They also had the drive, education, influence, and passion to paint a new one.

TRAPPED

In big and small ways, people who engage in mindful leadership training discover something more about themselves. Even in the small taste of training I was able to offer in the workshop, one participant made an important discovery. Nathan, a young businessman, sought me out the next day to share his experience of the workshop. He was smiling from ear to ear and began by saying, "I have to tell you that you changed my life." I can't be sure about that, but I do know, from my own experience as a vice president for more than fifteen years, that when good leaders are touched by something, they don't easily let it slip away. Here's Nathan's story.

> I had just settled into my chair with my laptop and phone so that I could tweet any memorable experiences in the workshop. I always do this in workshops and presentations. This is how I share the forum with people I know, so I wasn't very happy when you asked us to put down our laptops and shut off our phones. In fact, I was really quite angry, and my anger kept growing as you began to speak.
>
> I had decided that I was going to leave, that this wasn't for me, and since the room was so filled, no one would be bothered if I just sneaked out the back door. Just as I was reaching for my laptop on the floor, you asked everyone to be silent to begin the first meditation. Now I was trapped because I would make noticeable noise if I got up.
>
> I closed my eyes and started to listen to your instructions about meditation. At first, all I noticed was how angry I was and how my body felt tight and uncomfortable. But as the meditation continued, I noticed some softening, not only in my body but also in the anger itself. I became curious about what might happen next as the session continued, so I decided to stay even though I now had a chance to sneak out.

The next time we practiced, I was more at ease and noticed that I began to wonder how often my reaction to something that I don't expect, or am uncomfortable with, is to bolt. I wondered how often I might be missing something because I do. I've now committed myself to a journey to discover what happens if I don't bolt. What happens if I just stay curious? What might I discover?

Nathan came to Davos because he was interested in the big picture and the potential to have an impact on some of the complexities of today's world. He discovered in a mindful leadership setting that before we can discover the role we can play in a larger context, we first have to understand how our thoughts and emotions are influencing what we see and what we fail to see. Nathan, in just that one workshop, discovered something about himself that might have limited his potential to see clearly and to lead with excellence. As Nathan becomes more aware of his reactions to things that make him feel uneasy, he will be able to see more pieces of the big picture, and perhaps then see more opportunities to make a difference.

MINDFUL LEADERSHIP PRACTICES AND THE BIG PICTURE

It's easy to be pulled into the minutiae of your life and lose sight of the big picture. This is precisely where meditation practice and purposeful pauses can help pull you out of the details long enough to ask the important questions. As you become more familiar with noticing your thoughts, emotions, and bodily sensations, you begin to become more attuned to those situations where you are called to see the big picture before making a choice.

The stopping that results from choosing to practice, or taking a purposeful pause, can create the space you need to ask an important question, or make an important choice. It is also in this spaciousness that you are often reminded that the situation you find yourself in is not *win at all costs*, *all or nothing*, *black or white*, or *my way or the highway*.

The big-picture view reminds us of our connections, our responsibilities, and our vast capacity to be open-minded and compassionate. It reminds us of our capacity to make a difference.

For most of us, the opportunity to make a difference is what really gets us out of bed in the morning. We want our contribution to be about more than a paycheck or the next promotion. We want to know that what we do really matters—to some*one*, or to some*thing* bigger than ourselves. When we stop long enough to listen deeply, we can often feel this pull inside of us. Perhaps you have already been noticing it during your meditation practice. There is something familiar about this feeling, and it is very fundamental to who we are. It is fueled by our realization that the big picture is the one that shows us we are all connected, all a part of the same scene. This is true for everyone. We can each look for big and small ways to affect our world. When we are in positions of influence, we have the opportunity to use our education, creativity, and access to resources to truly make a difference in the world. It is a responsibility and a privilege of leadership.

CHAPTER 15

Reaching Your Potential to Lead

Everyone has inside of him a piece of good news. The good news is that you don't know how great you can be! How much you can love! What you can accomplish! And what your potential is!

ANNE FRANK

TRAINING YOUR MIND THROUGH mindful leadership meditations, reflections, and purposeful pauses can transform you into more of who you are. As this training becomes an integral part of your life, the resulting ripple effect has the potential to transform your organization and your community. I have seen this transformation in myself, in organizations whose employees I have taught, and on Institute retreats with leaders from around the world.

How does this transformation take place?

For most of us, it takes place little by little. We are first struck by the simple act of stopping. Although we may have a vague sense of our busy-ness, it isn't until we actually put down the electronics and the other distractions for a time that we begin to reinhabit our bodies and minds, and usually our hearts. Daily meditations invite us to regularly be in our own good company and, while we are, to notice more about how we are *really* doing—not how we think we're doing or how others think we're doing. We might notice exhaustion, aches and pains, unresolved thoughts, or unacknowledged emotions. We might stop long enough to be profoundly grateful for the life we have been given, and the many blessings we have within it. We might begin to notice conditioned behaviors that arise from our reactions to emotional or circumstantial triggers. Or we might begin to see the ways in which we are denying our principles or constantly ignoring the important things in life because something else seems more urgent at the time.

The life of the mind, which we have seen encompasses much more than the use of the analytical brain, becomes a new frontier to explore, and we find that discoveries await us every day. This exploration is not always a pleasure trip. Often, when we come face-to-face with ourselves, those around us, and the environment in which we live and work, we finally see things that we have successfully pushed away or ignored for a long time, sometimes decades. However, at the same time that we are developing this clarity and focus, we are also developing creativity and compassion. We discover our resourcefulness, and we experience the incredible moments of joy and peacefulness that have always been right here for us to experience, even though we rarely noticed them.

We can create the space to make intentional choices about what we discover, what we finally see. We can meet these discoveries with an openness and courage that can lead to creative solutions. Importantly, we have learned something more about the critical role of compassion in leading and living with excellence. Compassion allows us to understand the suffering around us as belonging to everyone, and our own suffering as a part of who we are that can be acknowledged and attended to, with kindness and gentleness.

As importantly, taking the time to train ourselves begins to offer us new ways of being in relationship to what we are discovering. We notice fear, and rather than bury it, we gently turn toward it and become accepting and curious about it. We learn how to see and accept the reality of today, just as it is.

THE NEXT STEP is to explore what, if any, choices might be wiser than those that you have historically made. So, for example, with fear, as you turn toward it and become curious about it, you might learn that you don't need to work so hard to distract yourself from the feeling, or you may come to understand that your fear is based upon an imagined set of consequences that are unlikely to occur.

As you experiment with embodying your practice, you quickly learn that a small change is often all that is necessary. Whether it is in offering an act of compassion to a difficult person in your life, or letting go of some of the storytelling that has kept you clinging to a lifestyle of too many meetings, or stepping beyond your smaller agendas to see the bigger picture, a small experiment can yield big changes. Mindful leadership does not ask you to change everything and everyone around you. It teaches you to be more fully aware of what is here, and invites you to experiment with intentional choices that make small changes. Your practices often allow you to see new, more skillful ways to meet each moment. You keep learning, and you keep strengthening and cultivating your innate ability to focus, see clearly, be creative, and embody compassion. These are the abilities that help you enhance your *capacity to connect* to yourself, others, and your community, and that help you enhance your *capacity to skillfully initiate change*—respectfully, collaboratively, and creatively.

THE EFFECT OF LEADERSHIP PRESENCE ON OUR WORLD

If you are in a position of influence, and therefore a leader, as we use the term in this book, then bringing the practice into your day-to-day responsibilities will quickly begin to affect others and affect the decisions you are making. Within just a few days of daily practice, you might see that you are more able to notice when you are not present, when you are just going through the motions, or only partially attentive to the moment, *and* you also might see that you have been using your training to redirect your attention to be attentive to the moment. That full attention will affect your experience of the day, and it will affect the experience of those interacting with you during the day.

Redirecting your attention also means that you will more consistently bring all of your capacity to the table, rather than 20 percent of it while the other 80 percent is split between thoughts of the past and thoughts of the future. When you bring all of your capacity, you also bring your leadership principles and your understanding of what is important. You listen to others with full attention; you notice the impulse to "check the box," and instead you choose to be courageous enough to hold the ambiguity of a novel situation for a time and wait for the dust to settle before making a choice. You more consistently embody *leadership presence*.

What is leadership presence?

It is each person's capacity to be fully present. We feel it, and others feel it. A leader who embodies leadership presence is:

Nonjudgmental
Open-minded
Open-hearted
Self-aware
Patient
Humble
Trusting
Collaborative
Compassionate

Sound familiar? You may have created a similar list from the Reflection on Leadership Excellence exercise in Chapter 3.

When we cultivate leadership presence, we are no longer solely concerned with the question "What do you want to do when you grow up?" We now are at least equally concerned with the question "Who do you want to be when you grow up?"

The first question, what we want to do, is finite and narrow and limited by the outside world. The second question, who we want to be, is infinite, inspiring, and completely an inside job. When we train our minds to cultivate focus, clarity, creativity, and compassion, we find the space to lead. And in that space we have the room to make choices that move us closer to who we want to be when we grow up.

One morning, I was reading an interview with James Hackett, the CEO of Steelcase. When he was asked about his most memorable leadership lessons, he mentioned that in the course of his work, he met many CEOs, and he noticed that the ones who were truly effective, genuine leaders in every sense of the word, were those who were not "prepackaged." The great leaders, in his view, were those who exhibited a "sense of peace, this self-awareness, which says, 'I understand who I am.'"

I was touched by his words and how strongly they resonated with my experiences over the past twenty-five years. On its face, the invitation to be self-aware and to embody your authenticity in the workplace seems simple. Just be yourself—sounds pretty easy, right?

We come to know from mindful leadership practice that becoming self-aware sounds simple, but it is not easy. Adding to the challenges of training the mind are the realities of evolving into a leadership role in today's world. On the path to becoming an influencer in many organizations and groups, you can be presented with enticing invitations to be like someone else, or moments that beckon you to ignore that gut feeling and step away from the values and ethics you hold deeply. There are the unwritten rules of the organization, the stories about the need to "manage up," the pressures of meeting this quarter's numbers, the calls to "do something" even when patience is the better course, and the statements about what "everyone" is doing in the marketplace as justification for actions that take you into gray areas. It takes strength and courage to stand in "who I am" at moments like this. The more time you spend in exploring and understanding yourself, the more likely you are to find that strength and courage. It is not easy, but the choice, it turns out, is simple. It is a simple choice because when you make choices that don't align with who you are, a little piece of you is lost, perhaps forever.

REFLECTION: WHO DO YOU WANT TO BE?

I guided a group of experienced leaders through this reflection at a refresher session for mindful leadership alumni and was deeply touched by the responses shared at the end of the session. It is a reflection that invites you to check in with yourself and see if you are who you want to be, living the life you want to live.

Take a comfortable seated posture with your feet flat on the ground and hands in your lap. Allow your eyes to gently close and begin to practice with your breath. As the body and mind settle into the silence, softly speak aloud the following sentence written by David Whyte:

There comes a time when you find that you've promised
yourself to things that are just too small.

What sensations, thoughts, and emotions arise? Which words resonate with you?

Remember that when you practice with a reflection, you may want to put aside the first one or two reflexive answers that arise and repeat the words of the sentence again, being open and curious about whatever arises.

Take your time. Feel free to go back to practicing with the breath if you find yourself engaging in assessments or analysis of what arises. When the mind becomes more focused, repeat the sentence again and see what arises.

Perhaps you heard the words *you find* as a reminder of how much more clearly we can see when we are present. Or perhaps those words reminded you that we can sometimes find insights by making room in our lives so we can notice our inner wisdom, rather than relying only on the discursive capacity of the mind.

Or perhaps you found yourself wondering about the definition of *small*. What is too small? Is it something that others told you to do? Or something that someone said you should do because you are good at it? Is it something that does not fully utilize your capabilities, or feed your passions? Or is it something so focused on the short-term results that it ignores the big picture?

You might have asked what makes something small. Are you attached to the status quo? Are you fearful? Would spaciousness lead to bigness? Is your role as a leader really about inviting this bigness?

What about *promised yourself*? Have you promised yourself to everything? To nothing?

Some of us have been on a prescribed trajectory all of our adult lives. Is it still the path that works? Are there aspects that are no longer—or never were—nourishing, or aligned with our principles and passions? If we are excited about the *what* of our work, do we need to change the *how*? Where are the win-win-win opportunities: good for the organization, good for the employees, good for the community? How do we lead in ways that are big?

When you are ready, spend some time writing about your responses.

> The act of writing can often help clarify and deepen the words and phrases that arise in a reflection. As you consider your writings, are there insights that lead you to a new choice? Have you promised yourself to things that are just too small? If so, what is one step toward something big that you will take this week?

THE RIPPLE EFFECT

I have one final thought to share with you. Never underestimate the ripple effect. Every person has the capacity to lead with excellence. Excellence in leadership comes from cultivating self-awareness and the space needed to make focused, clear, compassionate, and creative choices. Each choice you make has the potential to create a ripple effect that improves the status quo, and you rarely know just how far that ripple will travel.

Our world needs mindful leaders, people who embody leadership presence. We need leaders who not only understand themselves but who are not afraid to be open-hearted and who have the strength of character to make ethical choices. The problems we see all around us are not insurmountable, but they do require a new kind of leadership. As you continue to practice, and find more and more ways to actually be here for your life, you are also likely to encounter more and different ways to influence the lives of others, in your team, in your organization, in your families, and in your community. One small step changes the dance, and one small change has the potential to create a better world. The choice is yours. Enjoy the journey!

Acknowledgments

I never thought I would become a corporate officer, or develop and teach mindful leadership retreats and courses, or for that matter, write a book. And I wouldn't have, without the help, wisdom, and encouragement of many wonderful people. These people align along three major threads. When entwined together, these threads have brought me to this point in my life.

The first is my legal and leadership thread. My career was influenced by every colleague and client I encountered, thousands of wonderful people over the past twenty-five years. And every experience was a training ground for me to learn and to stretch. Although these people are too numerous to mention by name here, I want to extend my deep gratitude to all those who allowed me to be a part of the struggles and joys of leading in today's world.

The second thread is my mindfulness thread. I was fortunate to be introduced to mindfulness by Jon Kabat-Zinn and am grateful to Jon for his encouragement and support throughout the past decade. I am also deeply grateful to Saki Santorelli, who was a patient guide as my practice began to evolve, and who taught me the fine art of teaching mindfulness as we became partners in the development of the first mindful leadership retreats.

The retreats, courses, and ongoing support that are now the centerpiece of the Institute for Mindful Leadership were developed and refined as a result of the curiosity and candor of my colleagues at General Mills. I am very grateful to the officers, directors, and managers who explored mindful leadership training; who asked wonderful questions about their personal practice; and who shared their ideas and enthusiasm for bringing the training more fully into the challenges of leadership, and to all levels of the organization. It is a great honor to be a part of the journey with each of you.

Finding the courage to take the leap necessary to leave my position at General Mills and begin the nonprofit Institute for Mindful Leadership was made much easier with the support of dear friends. These were the people who believed in the mission of the Institute and were willing to help it become a reality: Susan Albers, Sandy Behnken, Vikram Ghosh, Jim Gimian, Autumn Huiras, Mariann Johnson, Florence Meleo-Meyer, and Terry Pearson. Thanks to all of you for holding firmly to that belief, especially in those times when my mind was filled with worry and doubt. And once the Institute became a reality, I had the good fortune to be surrounded by the talented members of the Institute's first board of directors: Patricia Barrick, Joe Ens, Jim Gimian, Peter Krembs, Anita Lauricella, and Peter Thompson. Thank you all for your invaluable guidance and generosity.

This book owes its existence to a skilled team of professionals. Thank you to Jim Gimian for his expert help and support in the book proposal stage and throughout the process. Thank you to Stephanie Tade, my agent, for making the connection to a great publisher, Bloomsbury Publishing. Thank you to Peter Ginna, my editor, for his insightful comments and suggestions and enthusiasm for the project. And thank you to the entire Bloomsbury team responsible for getting it into print and on the shelves, especially George Gibson, Rob Galloway, Nikki Baldauf, India Cooper, Laura Keefe, Summer Smith, Marie Coolman, Cristina Gilbert, and Derek Stordahl.

I want to extend a very special thank you to Barry Boyce, my development editor and friend, whose wise and supportive editing skill not only made the book better, but also turned this writing experience into a journey of exploration and learning. It was a privilege to work with someone who so clearly "walks the walk" of mindfulness.

The final of my three threads is the most long-lived and began with my loving parents, Joseph and Gloria Marturano, and my best friends, my brother Tom and my sister Diane. I have been blessed in many ways in my life but no blessing has been as meaningful as the blessing of being part of a loving family. Thank you to all of the members of the families to which I belong: Marturano, Thompson, Lauricella, Cioce, Gemborys, Capasso, and Dobroski. Your love and support is the fountain from which I have always drawn strength and courage.

The jewel around which these threads are wrapped is my immediate family: my spouse, Peter Thompson, and my children, Brian Marturano Thompson and Lauren Marturano Thompson. Thank you, Brian and Lauren, not only for keeping me supplied with green tea during long days of writing but for your enduring love and understanding.

To Peter, I have no words to adequately express the deep gratitude and love I feel for you. You have generously shared with me your love, your wisdom, your undying support, and your patience. Our lives, including this book and the work of the Institute, have evolved from our uncommon partnership. And none of this journey would have happened without you. I am eternally grateful.

Index to Meditations, Reflections, and Purposeful Pauses

Purposeful Pauses

Developing a Personalized Practice

WEEK	MEDITATIONS (minimum two 10-minute meditations/day)	PURPOSEFUL PAUSES	REFLECTIONS
1	Breath & Sound Meditation	Three per day	
2	Desk Chair Meditation	Three per day	What is leadership excellence?
3	Alternate between Breath & Sound and Desk Chair	Three per day	Calendar Reflection
4	•Mindful Communication: Listening to Yourself •Walking Meditation	Four per day (include Calendar Reflection)	Reflection on Inspiration

(continued)

WEEK	MEDITATIONS (minimum two 10-minute meditations/day)	PURPOSEFUL PAUSES	REFLECTIONS
5	Thoughts & Emotions Meditation	Four per day	What are your leadership principles?
6	•Mindful Communication: Listening to Others •Kindness Meditation	Five per day (include a Mindful Meeting)	Who (not what) do you want to be?
7 and beyond	Choose any two meditations daily. Increase practice time as you see fit.	Keep adding Purposeful Pauses (include Letting Go of Expectations)	Use reflection practice for any important question in your life.

Index

A Note on the Author

Janice Marturano is the founder and executive director of the Institute for Mindful Leadership, a nonprofit organization dedicated to training and supporting leaders in the exploration of mindfulness and leadership excellence. She founded the Institute for Mindful Leadership in December 2010, after ending her fifteen-year tenure as vice president, public responsibility, and deputy general counsel for General Mills, Inc.

While a corporate officer at General Mills, Janice codeveloped the very first mindful leadership curriculum at the University of Massachusetts Medical School's Center for Mindfulness where she served as a volunteer member of the advisory board. As a certified teacher of mindfulness and an experienced former officer of a Fortune 200 company, she has brought the intensive training of mindful leadership to leaders from all forms of organizations—corporate, nonprofit, academic, government, and military. In 2013, she taught an experiential mindful leadership workshop at the World Economic Forum in Davos, Switzerland.